HURDLES ARE F

By the same author

FOR GOD'S SAKE, DOCTOR!
THE MOON LOOKS DOWN

HURDLES ARE FOR JUMPING

FRANCES McALL

NEW CHERWELL PRESS · OXFORD

First published in Great Britain 1998
by New Cherwell Press
7 Mount Street, Oxford OX2 6DH
Copyright © 1998 F.McAll

British Library Cataloguing-in-Publication Data
A catalogue record for this book
is available from the British Library

ISBN 1-900312-20-4

Cover illustration by Steinar Lund
Cover design by Philip Carr
Printed by Biddles, Guildford

By my God have I leaped over a wall

Psalm 18 v 29

CHAPTER 1

Ken and I are both doctors. A year after our return from China, where we had spent four years of internment under the Japanese, we set up in general practice, operating from home. During the war we had lost most of our belongings several times over as well as our work as medical missionaries. The Mission had been unable to give us any pay for the time we had been interned, so our funds were low. There were twenty-seven courageous patients on our list when the National Health Service took over in 1948. Numbers rose steadily, a situation helped by the timely death of an uncle who bequeathed his patients to us and by the summer invasion of visitors to this seaside resort who obliged by lying too long in the sun, eating the wrong things or getting stung by wasps and other pests.

It was surprising to find ourselves in this position. Life had taken some odd twists and was to take plenty more in the years to come. We had expected to spend our lives working as doctors in a Mission hospital in China and living alongside Chinese. Both of us were sure this was what God wanted us to do. Instead we had spent most of our time since going to China shut up behind barbed wire with every variety of American and British passport-holder, all contacts with our Chinese friends being abruptly ended. Now China was closed to us since the Communists had taken over, and here we were involved in what I had always considered the lowest form of medical life, general practice in our own country.

Not only that but, being totally undomesticated, I was now having to run a home and feed a growing family. In China, on our meagre salary of two hundred pounds a year, we had been able to employ a cook and house-boy and I was exempt from all household chores. I had never cooked a meal in my life. In those days Domestic Science classes at school had only been for the non-academic and I had steadfastly avoided learning anything, apart from how to wash up, at home. My most success-ful dish proved to be a concoction of leftovers hotted up. It was known as 'Mother's mess'. That we had survived, not only physically but emotionally and spiritually as well, seems to us something of a miracle considering the hurdles along the way which could so easily have been our downfall. This is an autobiographical story, not always chronological, told in the hope that it may give hope to others.

CHAPTER 2

It is surprising that we married at all. That we have stayed married for over fifty years is even more surprising. We are an oddly assorted couple and look at many things from very different angles.

Ken is an artist with a lively imagination and the gift of 'seeing' things; a do-it-yourself man who would have made an ideal Stone Age husband; a do-it-now person with a zest for adventuring into unknown territory. The sign 'Trespassers will be prosecuted' is an open invitation to climb over the wall to see what's on the other side and why it should be forbidden. He scorns opposition as 'stupid' and presses ahead regardless of it. I love music but have little imagination. I am only practical if forced to be so and am only too ready to put off till tomorrow what does not have to be done today. I am a born sceptic, possibly the result of coming from a long line of lawyers, and I like to be liked so do not readily court disagreement. I find the thought of adventure more exciting in theory than in practice.

Ken throws nothing away. Anything — old shoes, perished hot water bottles, a bit of wire — might come in useful and, sadly, often does. Every empty space is there to be used and every empty pot, ornamental or otherwise, to be filled. I hate clutter and will happily chuck out anything which is not immediately useful or of great sentimental value. Ken likes the bedclothes loose and will often throw them off. I like to be tightly tucked in and kept warm. We both snore. Not very good grounds for marital bliss you might think.

There was a certain similarity in our backgrounds in that we both came from churchgoing families. Ken's family-tree boasted what must surely be a record number of people who had worked overseas as missionaries of one sort or another. His father was a surgeon in a mission hospital in China and had started, with another doctor, the first western-style medical school in the country. His mother was a midwife in the same hospital. Like her son, she revelled in spicy adventure. Obstetric emergencies in the surrounding villages provided this in plenty. On one occasion, having been threatened with having the house burned down round her if she failed to deliver a live male child — and this after the local 'midwife' had done her worst — she had to be wrapped up in paper like a parcel and smuggled out of the village slung from a pole borne between two men.

There was a certain amount of glamour in my mother's family. Three of her brothers had served in the Canadian Mounted Police. One had been a journalist reputed to have crawled through barbed wire with Churchill during the Boer War. She herself had longed to work abroad but was kept at home to look after the aunt who had brought her up. My father's family had been rooted in one area for several generations. Though far from being straight-laced they were eminently respectable even to the extent of his declaring with great solemnity that no one in the family had ever done anything foolish. My grandmother's servants were allowed to keep their jobs on condition they attended the evening service in church on Sundays and family morning prayers, led by grandfather, on weekdays.

For both of us, going to church was something not to be argued about. We just went. Ken, at a boarding school for sons of missionaries, got some satisfaction from pumping the organ and thereby avoiding having to put his precious penny in the collection. I amused myself during the thirty-minute sermon preached by our

4

eminent minister, by climbing, in my imagination, round the church planning the best route from gallery to gallery, while sucking licorice lozenges which were passed along the pew by father to keep us quiet.

Something must have rubbed off on us to be appreciated later. I certainly loved singing hymns, from the age when I had to stand on the pew to do so, and fell in love with the organ. At the age of seven I discovered that girls could be doctors and from then on it was assumed that I would be a medical missionary, partly inspired by the glamour of the 'returned' missionaries who stayed in our home. It never occurred to me that I might be a doctor in my own country. I think I had a sneaking feeling that I might not be good enough. Work in a Mission hospital might be less demanding. Little did I know. Ken, with less enthusiasm, also saw himself as returning to China to follow in his father's footsteps.

Teenage years came with their usual turmoil and challenges. For both of us, the Church seemed increasingly irrelevant with its large quota of old ladies occupying the pews. Yet, for me, whether God existed or not became the question which I could not drop. It would decide my whole future. Somehow I had to know. If I did not believe, how could I possibly be a missionary? Also, by now, music had become a strong contender for my ambitions. On the other hand, how could I possibly confess to my mother that I had doubts and was considering changing course? Both parents gave us amazing freedom to choose our own paths, but I could not face the pained look which would come over my mother's face. It was a lonely battle.

CHAPTER 3

Around this time, and five hundred miles apart, Ken and I both met up with the Oxford Group. This was a Christian group which made a profound impact in the twenties and thirties especially on students and youth of all kinds. Ken was by now a medical student in Edinburgh and I was in my last year at school. The Group's message was simple. With God's help, and accepting His standards, difficult human nature could be changed. He was still, in this day and age, ready and waiting to speak to anyone willing to listen and obey. 'He has a plan for everyone,' they said. This, for me, in my doubt-ridden and confused teens, was like a light being switched on. To them, God was very definitely alive and well.

Ken, after such a time of listening, felt as though a load had rolled off his shoulders as he posted off a parcel of books he had 'borrowed' from his old school. That very day he found himself helping an older man who had an alcohol problem which was threatening his marriage. This amazed Ken as much as it did the other man.

As I sat on the edge of my bed with pencil and paper, as they had suggested, I asked God, assuming He was there, to tell me what was stopping me from knowing Him. Immediately a thought like a no-nonsense but totally uncondemning voice came into my head: 'You are a very critical, superior person.' This took me completely by surprise. God was clearly ignoring the fact of my youthfulness. The jealousy I had for my much more popular sister then came uninvited into my mind. Telling her about this, having never confided such things to each other before, opened floodgates of confidence which have never closed. The fact that I was madly in love with a

married middle-aged man seemed of secondary importance to the Almighty, but it was a great relief to find
myself unexpectedly freed from its clinging
obsessiveness.

I struggled on, trying to listen to God's thoughts but
still feeling a barrier between me and Him, until one
evening, when a few of us were talking together, I
suddenly felt blanketed by an overwhelming love, as
though God Himself had put His arms round me. He felt
like the Jesus I had heard about all my life but had
ignored for so long. That day He became and remains
my closest friend.

So it came about that Ken, when he first heard of my
imminent arrival in Edinburgh to study medicine, was
sure God was telling him that I was the one he would
marry. I, on the other hand, was far from ready to be
anyone's wife. I was about to embark on a career of my
choice. It was, I thought, God's as well. I was enjoying
my freedom and, having grown up in a family of four
girls, was also enjoying mixing with an attractive assortment of young males. Marriage held no appeal for me.
I did not relish the thought of playing second fiddle in a
marriage situation, being just somebody's wife. And as
for 'sex', I did not see it as the most wonderful thing in
life. In fact I had a genuine fear of it taking over.

But I soon became painfully aware of Ken's brown
eyes following me round. Wherever I went he seemed to
be there too. If I saw him walking along the road, I
would hastily dodge down a side-street to avoid him. He
had not taken to the idea of being a medical missionary
as keenly as I had and I learned later that he had made
a bargain with God that he would carry out this plan and
go to China if God would permit him to marry me. He
still seemed to want me in spite of my poor response.

It soon became a matter of urgency as Ken was three years ahead of me and would soon be graduating and moving off. I was aware of this and, finally, in desperation, I got down on my knees and asked God what I was supposed to do. The answer came immediately and unexpectedly. That is, I expected Him to say simply: 'Marry Ken,' or: 'Don't marry Ken.' What he did say was: 'I want you to give all you can to Ken.' So that was it. That day, when I saw him walking along the road past the Students' Union, I ran to catch up with him and it seemed the most natural thing in the world to be doing so.

Ken's mother and the aunt who had been with them from infancy in China had set up home in a flat conveniently near the university and the infirmary where his two sisters were training as nurses. I now became a regular visitor and was accepted as an unofficial member of the family.

Ken's remarkable father, a keen archer and tennis-player, who had spent the last thirty years in China translating medical text books into Chinese, came home about the time that Ken graduated. He had missed all his children's teenage years. His first act was to visit a hospital consultant who confirmed what he already suspected, that he had a life-threatening heart condition. Sadly he kept this from the family who misunderstood his eagerness to attend every possible lecture and film available, thinking all this rather boring.

Ken went off to a hospital job in my home town where we were able to get together during my holidays. The girls were busy and tired with their nursing activities; so, feeling sorry for their father, it was left to me to accompany him whenever I had time. There was a certain element of wanting to impress him in my motives, but these are memories which I greatly treasure.

When his illness became apparent to everyone, the family rallied round. His last few months were perhaps the richest we had experienced together and we were able to appreciate to the full his faith and the humour which bubbled up from the depths.

Almost to the end he was busy compiling a Chinese medical dictionary, quizzing me whenever I came in about any new term or condition I might have learned about that day. He would sit in his dressing gown, keeping a catapult and a jar of peas at his side to shoot at any unfortunate pigeon daring to perch on the tree outside the window. I don't remember him hitting any of them. He died in March '37 having lived longer than expected. I can still feel the drama of giving my very first injection to him a few days earlier.

In September that year Ken got the train from the old Princes Street station, and that was the last we would see of each other for two years — two years during which, quite apart from the difficulty of writing adequate letters which took six weeks to get through, many things, both personal and in the world, happened which could easily have separated us for good but somehow failed to do so.

CHAPTER 4

At the time I graduated in 1939 it was enough to pass the Final exams to be thrown out on to the world as a fully fledged doctor. It was the 'done thing', but not compulsory, to spend time working in various hospital departments for a year or more to gain experience. For me, the important thing was to get to China as soon as possible. To fill in the time it took to make all the necessary arrangements and to be interviewed and officially accepted by the Mission, I took a job as a locum in a general practice in the East End of London.

I could hardly have been thrown into a tougher situation. The doctor disappeared the moment I arrived, leaving me totally on my own. His housekeeper, who seemed to be the only person in Britain at that time to be expecting imminent war with Germany, said she would lie down flat in the middle of the road if an aeroplane flew over. She kept the linoleum-floored waiting room gleaming, but the consulting room she dared not touch. This hardly surprised me as every available space was occupied by unopened advertisements, journals and samples. Dusty ancient bottles with impressive Latin labels filled the shelves along one wall.

But the real work was done behind a screen. Here stood a green baize-covered card-table on which were seven large Winchester jars holding all that was necessary for day-to-day treatment of constipation, diarrhoea, insomnia, coughs or anaemia. Employed patients could get their consultations and prescriptions free 'on the panel'. Others had to pay. It cost one shilling and sixpence for a consultation and two shillings for a home visit. For these, I would retire behind the screen, scratch my head and select what seemed most appropriate. A prescription made up by the chemist would be more than most could afford. I kept a duster with me to use between consultations. I too did not dare move anything. The salary of eight pounds a week seemed a fortune.

The previous year the Oxford Group had launched a campaign for 'Moral and Spiritual Rearmament' to counter the military build-up then underway to meet the growing threat from Hitler. East London had been chosen for this occasion and when I arrived there the campaign was in full swing. I joined in, visiting schools and factory canteens in the lunch hour. It was an exciting and exhilarating experience and amazingly full of fun. Many people had given up their jobs to do this and every penny that turned up to support them seemed like a miracle. It was like living in the first days of the early church.

It was here that I met Annie. She was a rugged little lady from the north who, whenever I met her, always made me feel I wanted to be my best. She had sold her millinery business for £40 to come and work with her son who was helping to lead this campaign. It was her total capital and I remember overhearing on one occasion that she and Bill at that moment had precisely sixpence between them. It did not appear to be worrying them.

One day she showed me her hands, gnarled and misshapen from arthritis. She had realised just that morning that, for the past eighteen months since she had decided to drop years of bitterness and let God into her life, she had had no more pain. She had been so busy she had not even noticed the miracle. This was my first introduction to such happenings. I carried a photo of her radiant face and memories of those days with me through the difficult days of the war.

People said, 'How foolish you are to be going to a

country where there's a war on.' Japan had invaded China two years earlier. But on August 4th, 1939, I sailed on the P&O Cathay to the usual heart-rending accompaniment of streamers thrown from ship to shore gradually breaking as the ship pulled away from the dockside, my parents getting smaller with every minute. I retired to my bunk feeling sick. By the next morning my love of the sea had taken over. I was due to arrive in Shanghai early September.

The first crisis arose when my writing case containing my passport vanished. I was summoned to the Captain's cabin where I was told by a senior army officer how foolish I was to leave it lying around. There was, apparently, a roaring trade in British passports at that time. A secret search of every cabin was to be made forthwith. Fortunately, before this could happen, the case turned up under a cushion in the lounge. The shadow of our own war suddenly became real. It became even more real when, on arriving in Bombay, the ship was ordered back to Britain and all passengers turned off.

This did not immediately affect me as I had arranged to spend two weeks with my sister and brother-in-law who were working in a mission hospital in south India. The plan was that I would then pick up another boat from Colombo, on which would be my heavy luggage. While I was with them, war broke out in Europe and a cable came from our Mission in London which read: 'All ships cancelled. Find your own way.' This was some-what daunting for a twenty-three year old girl in a strange country.

Pleasant though it was staying with my sister and two small children whom I was meeting for the first time, it seemed a good idea to make my way to Madras where there was a P&O office. There were friends in Madras with whom I could stay. I went to the office as soon as I arrived. The young clerk's jaw dropped. 'The *Viceroy of India* sailed from Colombo yesterday' he said. 'We didn't know she was coming and we don't expect any other.' At least my sheets and blankets were on their way to China.

When I had recovered my equilibrium, he advised me to go to Calcutta where there would be a chance of picking up one of the British India Line boats which carried cargo and a few passengers between South Asian ports and Shanghai. My Madras friends contacted the Bishop of Calcutta who was in the habit of taking in strays and he agreed to put me up for as long as was necessary. This meant a two-day train journey all by myself in an 'Intermediate' carriage. This was considered necessary for my safety as a white girl, but the sight of the milling throngs climbing on to the train at every station made me long to join them. Just as I was feeling at my most abandoned, the train stopped at a tiny country station. On a newspaper stand in the middle of the platform was a small bright blue book with the title 'Moral Rearmament' written by a British tennis hero of my generation, 'Bunny' Austin. How it got there I will never know, or whether I dreamed it, but I no longer felt alone. In fact I laughed at the unlikeliness of it in that place

Something even more familiar and unexpected greeted me in Calcutta. Yet another sister, Margie, had joined the 'Cathay' in Marseilles and we had parted in Bombay. She was due to meet her fiancé in Kashmir and they planned to get married before going on to Burma where her husband-to-be had been appointed chaplain to the Bishop of Rangoon. But here she was at the station to greet me, with the wedding — to be performed by the

Bishop of Calcutta — only four days away. Here I was, just in time to be her bridesmaid.

After the wedding in the Cathedral, John and Margie took off for Burma. My sense of desolation returned. Each day I contacted the P&O office in the city but they knew nothing of any boats due to arrive. There was a blackout of information. I shared a large room in the Bishop's palace with two girls who were working with MRA, one of whom I had met before. This certainly helped, and our friendship grew as we all went down with 'break-bone' fever — Dengue, to give it its proper name — and lay side by side sweating it out and watching the lizards as they chased the culpable mosquitoes across the ceiling.

CHAPTER 5

Dengue was not the only affliction to hit me in Calcutta: I also acquired amoebic dysentery, one of the scourges of India, which must have accounted for much of the ill-health and lack of energy in the country. It was to haunt me for the next six years. To make a definite diagnosis the doctor needed a specimen to send to the laboratory. I had some difficulty in explaining to one of the Bishop's immaculately turbaned, white-clad servants what it was I needed for the purpose but eventually he vanished into the nether regions to reappear some time later with a large handsome cut-glass jar.

Days lengthened into weeks and still there was no sign of a ship. Meanwhile my education continued. It was not comfortable being British in the days of the British Raj. We swam in a magnificent swimming pool but the delight for me was modified by the notice at the gate, 'For Europeans only.' There were two-coach trams but one coach was reserved for whites only and was often empty while the other was crowded to overflowing. One day I was taken to the ultramodern Medical Research Institute and shown one of the first-ever Geiger counters, a very costly affair. From there we went on to watch the daily ritual outside the huge gates of a local Prince's palace where, at midday, over a thousand beggars would gather to receive a pittance of food through a hole by the gate. Many of the beggars were blind and many without limbs and I was told that parents often deliberately mutilated their children to make them more effective beggars.

My guide on this sightseeing tour was an Indian businessman in his late twenties. He was clearly a very bright young man. When I questioned him about his job, he told me, without any apparent resentment, that he had already risen as high as he could in the business because all top management had to be in the hands of a white Britisher. This may have been perfectly correct procedure but, for some reason, it got under my skin. In a beautiful park in the midst of this mixed-up, lovable city sat Queen Victoria on her throne whilst, at a busy road-junction near the station, two policemen stood one at each end of a somnolent cow directing the traffic round her.

One afternoon, an English tea-planter took a small party of us out to his home in the plantation several miles outside Calcutta on the edge of the jungle. As we sat drinking his excellent Indian tea, we listened to all the animal noises one associates with Kipling's *Jungle Book*. We traced the origin of a great deal of the noise when he took us to a ruined temple completely overgrown with creepers and now home to a huge colony of monkeys. All of them, apart from a few elderly ones who sat glaring at us through fiery eyes, seemed to be constantly on the move, swinging on the long trailing creepers from corner to corner of the ancient building, screeching at the tops of their voices as they did so.

Near the plantation was a village where we watched men sitting cross-legged on their doorsteps, as they sewed fine embroidery on ladies' underwear. This apparently was a project initiated by a group of socially-minded Calcutta ladies to help the poor villagers. Right next to the houses, themselves in considerable need of repair, were overgrown banana groves with their fences broken down because no one had the time or energy to look after them.

Still no ship arrived to take me on my way. All sorts of doubts, at which I hardly dared look, began to filter into my mind. I had always found it hard to let other people in on what I was thinking and feeling but apparently I was not as successful at hiding things as I imagined. One morning one of the girls, Peg, said, 'You're not happy are you?' I could hardly say that I was. She then suggested that we should go into the adjoining bathroom where we were unlikely to be disturbed. There were two hard chairs on which we sat while I waited for her to start asking probing questions but no questions came. After several minutes of silence, my friend quietly got up and, without a word, left the room closing the door behind her. I call her my 'friend' because no one could have done more for me at that moment than she did.

Left alone, I sat and stared out of the open window at a tall palm tree: its image is indelibly printed on my memory. All the uncomfortable thoughts I had been refusing to look at began to crystallise. The nagging question in my mind was whether this hold-up was God's way of telling me that I was on the wrong track. Was He trying to stop me from going to China? Did He after all not want Ken and me to marry? We had felt we were following His direction but motives can get very mixed up. Was I meant to go home and join the war effort? Did He want me to stay in India and work as my friends Erica and Peg were doing? I strongly suspected that this was what they were thinking though neither of them had said as much. If the answer to any of these questions was 'yes' how would people react? What would the Mission think? What would my family or Ken's family think? Above all, what would Ken think? Might he even be driven to suicide? My vanity suggested that this was a distinct possibility. If I went ahead with my original plans, how would Peg and Erica react? Their opinion had begun to matter to me very much.

All my life so far my greatest desire had been to please people and to be approved by them. Up till now this had not proved too difficult or so I thought. Now it seemed abundantly clear that in life one could not please everyone all the time and that to obey God might at times mean risking many prized relationships.

At the age of sixteen I had had that overwhelming experience of God's love and Presence which had made any future doubts about His existence impossible. I longed sincerely to pass this sureness on to other people. Now I seemed to be facing not a gentle, comforting Presence, but an almighty God who was asking me very clearly whether I was going to spend the rest of my life depending on the good opinion of others or simply live to please Him and to do what He wanted regardless of what people thought. I found I dared not leave that bathroom until I could with total honesty say 'Yes' to that.

I am not sure how long I sat on that chair. It could have been two hours or more. No one interrupted me. I squirmed and I wept. The palm tree outside the window stood straight and silent. Each time I almost reached the point of decision my nerve failed me. Finally, summing up every bit of courage I could muster, and it seemed very small indeed, I said, 'All right, God.' I had hardly come out with it before the clear thought came into my mind, 'Go ahead.' It came with such quiet certainty that I had no doubt at all where it had come from.

I almost danced out of the bathroom. All the load of doubt and depression seemed to have slid off my back. I didn't have to say anything to the other two girls: they just seemed to know without being told. The very next morning came a call from the shipping office telling me to get ready to leave at once. A ship had arrived and was due to sail within a few hours.

CHAPTER 6

The *Sirdhana* was a small coastal vessel belonging to the British India Company and plied between Calcutta and Shanghai. Mainly designed to carry cargo, she also had room for a handful of paying passengers. I had a tiny, second class cabin to myself and was waited on by a fatherly Indian steward who, every morning, brought me a cup of tea and news that my bath was ready and waiting for me. I have never had such attention before or since.

As soon as we had left the muddy waters of the Howrah river, awnings went up on deck and a small canvas swimming pool was erected. In this we — first and second class passengers alike — spent much of our time. Now the war, which had faded into the background during the weeks in Calcutta, became a stark reality. We were heading for Rangoon and rumours were rife that one of the German pocket battleships was prowling about in the Bay of Bengal which we had to cross. The Captain had been ordered to steer a zigzag course day and night. On our first day we had lifeboat drill which was to become a daily exercise from then on.

After dark the ship was blacked out and only the dimmest of lights allowed in the saloons and cabins. This made reading impossible and playing cards was difficult. We compensated for this by talking. Three of my fellow second class passengers were young Canadian doctors, two of them women, who were returning to Canada after several years working in Mission hospitals in India. The Captain, when he was free in the evenings, took to settling down with us and, though claiming to be a total unbeliever, delighted in plunging us into deep theological discussions. It seemed that, in spite of his professed atheism, he could not stop talking about God. When Sunday came round we found there were no plans for a service on board so asked if we could run one ourselves. 'Yes,' said the Captain, 'provided there's none of your "Peril on the sea" stuff'. If he could have known what lay ahead he might have felt differently.

One evening, when we were about half way across the Bay and in the middle of a lively debate, the third officer shouted down the companionway to the Captain to come at once to the bridge. He leaped from his seat and stumbled up the stairs out into the pitch dark and we followed. There was absolute silence on deck, the ship's engines hardly turning over. The sea was dead calm and very black. Suddenly, out of the darkness shone a brilliant light which blinded us and seemed to envelop the whole ship. We stood holding on to the ship's rail as though it could protect us, and I remember grinning fatuously at the light hoping this would soften the hearts of anyone out there who might have hostile intentions. At the same time we couldn't help wondering what it would be like when the torpedo struck.

After what seemed an eternity, a light from our bridge shone out in a series of dashes and dots. The searchlight went out and a flashing light took its place to be replaced once again by total darkness. We retreated, shaken, back to the saloon where, shortly afterwards, the Captain rejoined us. We had apparently been spotted by a British destroyer which was anxious to identify us. It had already asked for our name and nationality but, in the confusion on the dark bridge, our signal lamp had been kicked over and it took several precious minutes of crawling about on hands and knees before anyone could find it and give the required answer. During those moments of silence, we were probably in real danger of being torpedoed by the wrong side. No one was yet used to being at war. In the days that followed, lifeboat drill took on a new significance as did our discussions about God. We felt much cheered by the arrival of a turtle dove on the stern rail who travelled with us as far as the mouth of the Irrawaddy river.

By this time the Captain had become a firm friend. When we docked in Rangoon, he offered to take me by taxi to Bishopscourt where, I reckoned, Margie and John should by now be living. He said the boat might be held up for several days so, if they could have me, I could stay ashore and he would come and collect me when she was due to sail.

Arriving at Bishopscourt I was met by a servant who told me that John and Margie had been away and had arrived back only the previous day. Margie, he told me, was upstairs in her bedroom, first door on the right. With this reassurance the Captain left me to get back to the ship while I crept upstairs wanting to take Margie by surprise. This I did. She was sitting doing her hair, so the first sight of me was in her mirror. She looked as though she had seen a ghost. Once again she was picturing me safely in China or at least well on the way. Once again, also, the war receded as we caught up with each other's news.

Then I had the great pleasure of meeting Bishop West himself. I was beginning to feel more at ease with Bishops and he certainly made me feel very much at home. The next few days were spent sightseeing in this exotic city of sarongs, temples and saffron-robed monks. Bishopscourt itself stood next door to a Buddhist monastery and, only recently, the Bishop had opened a small gate in the fence which separated them, so that now there was a frequent coming and going between the two. The

Abbot and the Bishop had become close friends. At night, in bed, I lay listening to the gentle tinkle of the hundreds of tiny bells which surrounded the monastery roof. One of the Bishop's friends was the manager of the huge oil refinery by the river. Not everyone has the privilege of being shown round such a place. The experience came in useful years later when, as a GP in England, I needed to picture the conditions under which some of my patients worked in the local refinery. Next to the refinery and an offshoot of it, was a factory where candles were made, anything from tapers to candles several feet high and elaborately ornamented for use in churches or temples. Most of the workers, I noticed, were women.

When we were talking together one evening, the Bishop suggested that I might stay on a little longer in Rangoon and go on by flying-boat to Hong Kong. He was sure I would find some way of getting to Shanghai from there. Passenger flights were still in their infancy and the very thought of flying stirred up a host of butterflies in my insides. However, as the suggestion came from such a man as the Bishop, I felt I should give it full consideration. To change plans at this stage, apart from being very expensive, seemed a complicated thing to do and, in spite of what the Bishop said, uncertain to say the least. I did not want to risk any more delays. I was loath too, to break the contact with the Captain and my friends on board when we all seemed to be getting on so well. The more I thought about it the more I felt convinced it was right to stay with the ship and no one questioned my decision. Whether I was guided by fear or by God at that moment, I cannot be sure even now.

CHAPTER 7

On a glorious evening one week later, the Captain came to call for me. Margie, John and the Bishop escorted us to the jetty where a small launch was waiting to take the Captain and me to the *Sirdhana* which had already sailed and was now well down river.

On the jetty was a Chinese lady to whom I was introduced. She was the wife of a diplomat and claimed to be a close friend of Madame Chiang Kai Shek. When she heard I was going to China, she made me promise that I would introduce myself to Madame Chiang when I arrived. Sadly the opportunity never came my way but her insistence made me feel comfortably important and involved with China which I longed to be.

We climbed aboard the ship, which had slowed down for us. Ahead of us was the most magnificent sunset I have ever seen. The whole sky seemed to be ablaze and, looking back, we were blinded by the dazzling gold of the great Shwe Dagon pagoda as the setting sun caught it. All that now stood between us and Shanghai was about ten days' sailing interrupted by one day in Penang and another in Singapore. As I shaded my eyes to look at the glorious sky I felt a surge of excitement and, having also enjoyed meeting up again with my Canadian friends, was very glad I had decided to come back to the ship and finish the journey by sea. All seemed very well with my world at that moment.

Once out in the open sea again, the zigzagging continued but we hardly noticed it now except for the few minutes during which I was invited to take the wheel. Steering a large ship is not as easy as it looks and we left a very wavy wake astern. The heat soon drove us back into the pool again but as it was a very small pool, we had to take turns at splashing about in it. Then there were more deck games, more singing round the piano and, of course, more evening discussions with the Captain.

At one point he casually mentioned that, when he had reported to the shipping office in Rangoon, he was told that mines had now been laid outside Singapore harbour. He assured us that he had carefully entered their position on the appropriate chart as soon as he had got back on board. I remember feeling somewhat shaken that Singapore, such a bastion of empire, needed to be protected in this way but soon put it out of my mind as the evening's discussion became more absorbing.

Penang I remember mainly for bananas and snakes. It was, and still is, surprising to see that bananas grow upside down. As for snakes, there was something repulsive about the famous snake temple where the many images and every piece of furniture were garlanded with snakes, making everything appear to be writhing. I was glad to get out. But the atmosphere of the tropics really gripped me that day and has never loosed its hold.

Two days later we arrived in Singapore. It was a Sunday morning. My two Canadian friends and I were determined to make the most of the time ashore but, just as we were about to take off down the gang-plank, I was told that someone was looking for me. Turning back I was met by a smiling Chinese man. He introduced himself as Thio Chan Bee, a teacher in a Baptist school in the city who had heard from the Bishop of Rangoon that I would be passing through. I felt quite overwhelmed by his kindness.

Leaving my friends to go sightseeing on their own, I went off with Chan Bee. First he took me to visit his school, closed of course as it was Sunday, and then on

25

through the heart of the Chinese part of the city to his home. The Chinese, living so far away from their own country of origin, seemed determined to preserve all they could of their ancient culture. It was more traditional than China itself, abounding in curved-roofed temples, bright scarlet banners and the exotic smell of incense, I felt a most unworthy VIP as I was welcomed into Chan Bee's family and treated to my first genuine Chinese meal, waited on by his wife.

After lunch I was taken off by an old English friend from my home town, Conrad, who was now a magistrate in Singapore. He drove a red sports car of which he was inordinately proud, and in this he whisked me off on a lightning tour which included a drive through the magnificent botanical gardens and then back to his luxurious bungalow for a very English afternoon tea.

When I was finally deposited back at the ship it was to find that, while we had been away, it had filled up with hundreds of Chinese deck passengers. They were noisily settling down under a huge awning on the lower stern deck. Here they would sleep and eat, preparing food on their own small cooking stoves. It was a cheap way of travelling.

We were also told that twelve convicted criminals being deported to China, and said to be violent, had come on board. They were kept locked up in the foc's'le and guarded by soldiers from an Indian regiment. A few cabin passengers had also joined us including two Chinese girls who had taken over the cabin next to mine.

As usual, back on board, I locked my valuables away in my suitcase. These included my passport, which I had no intention of losing again, my purse and the gold watch which my parents had given me on my twenty-first birthday. For some reason it had stopped and, as I had already learned to do when anything went wrong, I was going to wait until Ken was around to put it right.

There was no discussion that evening as the Captain was too busy getting ready to sail early next morning. The two female Canadians and I decided on an early bed as we wanted to be up in good time to witness our departure, always an exciting moment on a sea voyage.

CHAPTER 8

We seemed to be the only passengers awake as we stood on the narrow deck immediately below the bridge, overlooking the forward deck with its cargo holds now covered over and battened down. From where we stood we could see the door leading into the foc'sle in which the criminals were held, an Indian soldier sleepily on duty outside. It was a beautiful morning, already warm, as we gazed at the offshore islands and the open sea beyond. We watched the pilot come aboard and make his way to the bridge. Ropes were heaved off bollards on the quay side, splashing into the water before being pulled onboard, and the ship slowly drew away. With nothing now between me and China, I was at last free to feel excited.

Singapore was beginning to look small in the distance when the pilot clambered down the ship's ladder into the small launch which had come alongside to pick him up. There was a farewell hoot from the *Sirdhana*'s siren and we were on our own. Within minutes we had changed course. This seemed odd, as one would expect a pilot to put us on course before leaving, but presumably the Captain knew what he was doing. It was just good to be on the move again with the end of the journey, which had already taken far too long, now in sight. It was good too, to feel that we were moving away from the threat of German ships and could, from now on, travel safely in a straight line. Japan was not to become a menace for another two years.

Suddenly, from somewhere ahead and below us on the port side, came a loud booming noise. At the same moment the bow of the ship was lifted upwards and sideways out of the water, making us grab at the rail to keep our balance. A huge spurt of oily water gushed up from beneath us, drenching us from head to foot as it came down again. We learned later that a large ventilator cowl from the lower deck had also shot up past us and had landed on the bridge just over our heads. It must have missed us by two or three feet. For the next few months I would jump every time a door banged or someone dropped something but at that moment we didn't wait to see what would happen next. Already the ship's siren was bleating and the ship itself was starting to go round in circles like a mad thing totally out of control.

We made a dash for our cabins and, by the time I reached the narrow passage leading to mine, the floor was at an odd angle, sloping downwards and to the left. As soon as I turned the handle the cabin door opened and I fell inside. Recovering my balance, I tried to remember what we had been told to do in an emergency which we never expected to happen. The two essentials, lifejacket and sun helmet, were lying ready to hand. I opened the cupboard by my bunk and seized my handbag. Catching sight of my much-prized Rollicord camera, I grabbed that too. Then, with a last look round at the little cabin which had been such a happy home for the past few weeks, I bolted back along the passage.

As I struggled, uphill now, towards the stairs leading to the deck, I remembered the two Chinese girls in the cabin next to mine who had only just come aboard and would not know what to do. I staggered back to find their cabin door locked and no amount of banging and shouting produced any response. I had no idea whether they were inside or not but dared not wait any longer to find out.

Climbing up the tilted companionway was extremely

difficult by now and by the time I got back on deck there was pandemonium everywhere except at our own boat-station where only the three Canadians were quietly waiting. Our boat had not yet been lowered from the boat-deck above us. People were clambering up from the lower decks and pouring across to the starboard side where they could see lifeboats being lowered. Because of the now severe list of the ship to port, the crew were trying to get the starboard boats down first before it became impossible to do so, but the hundreds of deck passengers who had had no lifeboat drill, and others who sadly should have known better, were hurling themselves on these boats, all of which tipped up and, still hanging crazily from their davits, emptied their contents into the sea.

In contrast, at our own boat-station on the port side there was an extraordinary calm. Our lifeboat was being held steady, just out of reach, until orders should be given to lower it and start loading. Time seemed to stand still and I sat down on a bench with a strange feeling of detachment. It was difficult to think seriously about the situation or to believe it was really happening. I had to make myself think that, if I died, that would be all right, and that if I lived then God must have some reason for that too. At that moment I was strangely unaware of all fear and was even able to pray for the terrified people who seemed, with all their clamour, so far removed from us. One Chinese woman's face still clings to my memory with its frozen look of terror. I longed to stop her in her headlong rush but she was too far away and soon out of sight.

At last an officer arrived at our station and immediately took control. Our boat was lowered to our deck level and suddenly people appeared from nowhere to clamber into it. In no time it had far more people in it than it was built to hold. I looked at the sea, far down below. It was calm, I knew it would be warm and I was quite proud of my swimming ability, so I was perfectly willing to jump into it and trust to being picked up later.

The boat had reached the level of the deck below before the officer noticed me still standing there, my camera slung over my shoulder and my handbag in one hand. He was clearly annoyed and told me to jump at once. I pointed out that there was no room for anyone else and that I was quite prepared to swim but he ignored this. Grabbing my arm and forcing me to the side of the ship, he seized my camera and hurled it unceremoniously on to the deck saying, 'No room for that,' then once more ordered me to jump. I looked down at the sea of faces with hardly an inch between them and jumped, saying 'Sorry' rather feebly as I landed on top of them.

The lifeboat was now hanging just opposite the saloon and, through the doorway, I could see, propped up on the music stand of the open piano, my precious copy of Elgar's *Dream of Gerontius*.

CHAPTER 9

The ship now looked enormous as it towered or rather leaned over us. I remembered that it was important to get away from a sinking ship as quickly as possible to avoid being sucked down with it. As I was wondering how we would achieve this, two tough-looking Chinese youths started pushing and shoving to try and get at the oars lying somewhere in the bottom of the boat. Packed like sardines as we were, it was no mean feat to extract them and get them into their rowlocks. One American lady had to be forcibly heaved out of their way as she screamed hysterically to her journalist husband, who was still on board the ship taking last-minute photographs as she went down.

It was a Herculean task for the two rowers to pull the boat away from the side but gradually the gap between us and the ship got wider and we could now see her whole length. The bows were already under water and the stern was rising higher and higher in the air. It was black with people. I have no idea how many finally escaped. It looked impossible.

It was then that I became aware of a slight movement under my feet. With much elbowing we managed to clear a small space through which we could see the figure of a Chinese woman lying on the bottom of the boat. She was alive but groaning and all we could do was to give her the smallest of breathing spaces and get our feet off her, not an easy thing to accomplish.

By this time one or two other lifeboats which had got away safely were bobbing around nearby, each with more than its full complement of occupants, and life-rafts were still being pushed off the ship into the sea. We watched as a small group of ship's officers lost their balance on the steeply sloping deck and slid unceremoniously on their backsides into the water. Only minutes later, exactly twenty minutes after the explosion in fact, the *Sirdhana* slipped forward and downwards and disappeared, a whirlpool of water closing over her. With her went an unknown number of nameless people.

It was now about ten o'clock and the sun beat down on us out of the cloudless tropical sky. We were grateful for the order to wear our unsightly sun helmets and felt sorry for those who had nothing to cover their heads with. Boats of varying sizes began to come out from Singapore and it seemed strange that they only came so far and no further, leaving us to go on roasting in the sun. Only later did we realise that, as we were still in the middle of the minefield, no one was going to come too close. The young Chinese rowed manfully and remarkably cheerfully until, at last, we emerged into safe waters where we were quickly surrounded by a host of motor launches and other craft.

One of the first boats to come anywhere near was a long boat from a Japanese vessel with a highly disciplined crew rowing her. They went round picking people out of the water or off the somewhat precarious life-rafts. Looking back it seems strange that we should live to be grateful to the Japanese for coming to our rescue.

Our own first visitor was a police launch. As soon as it came alongside, our two staunch rowers pulled in their oars, scrambled over us and were hauled aboard the launch and bundled down below before we had any opportunity to thank them. Until that moment we had not suspected that they were two of the violent criminals who had been shut up in the foc'sle. We learned later that two of the men in there had been killed by the explosion and that the guard had fled, leaving the rest locked up. They had been released in the nick of time by an officer of the regiment who had fired at the lock with his revolver.

We told the police about the Chinese woman under our feet and with great difficulty managed to lift her out and pass her over into their waiting arms. She was still groaning but barely conscious.

Then came the welcome sight of the Captain. He had been one of the group we had seen sliding down the deck of the ship just before she sank and we had feared for his safety. He had been picked up off a raft and was doing the rounds checking on survivors. He seemed relieved to see us but was particularly concerned for his chief engineer who was later found to be safe.

As he stood in his wet clothes, trying to keep his balance in the small motor boat and talking about what had happened, a man who had overheard our discussions in the saloon turned to me and said scornfully, 'Now what about your God and His guidance?' To my amazement and before I could think of anything to say, the Captain, going red in the face, leaped, not to my defence but to God's, tearing strips off the surprised man for daring to talk like that. It was an unforgettable scene out there on the open sea with a newly sunk ship only yards away.

CHAPTER 10

After an hour or more, we were transferred to a pleasure launch, one of several which came out to us just as soon as they knew it was safe to do so. We were an odd-looking lot. Most people were still in their night clothes, a few decently attired in dressing gowns with sun helmets on their heads. The two Canadian girls and I were covered in oil and our hair looked like well-greased rats' tails.

On this boat we were offered towels and given welcome cups of coffee. We were then kept waiting another two hours or so while, on shore, there was furious activity as the authorities worked out what to do with us. After being allowed ashore we were taken to the famous Raffles Hotel and ushered like honoured guests into its stately foyer. The three of us were given a three-bedded room with its own bathroom, a great luxury in those far-off days, where we were able to do something, though not very much, about our appearance.

News of the disaster had spread rapidly through the city and by the time we arrived in the hotel, the beds were already covered with an assortment of garments sent in by charitable local residents. Sadly they all seemed to have been created for outsize ladies, which none of us happened to be, and most of them were under-garments hardly needed in that climate. I particularly remember the largest pair of corsets I have ever seen which we wrapped twice round one of the girls. The horror of what we had just been through was temporarily forgotten as we paraded in front of the large mirror. It was my first, though not my last, taste of being on the receiving end of charity, not an easy position to be in when your need is great although you cannot bring yourself to be critical of the givers. On this occasion, as there was nothing we could wear, we stayed as we were.

At first I thought of changing some money and going out to buy clothes but when I looked in my handbag, to which I had clung as though my life depended on it, all that was in it was a bunch of keys belonging to my luggage which was now at the bottom of the sea and an expired driving licence. Then, of course, I remembered I had locked everything of value away in my suitcase in my cabin.

The others were no better off. Help came from an unexpected source. Conrad, my magistrate friend, had just arrived in his office when he heard what had happened and had immediately abandoned his work to come dashing in his car down to the hotel to find out if I had survived. Having found me there with my two friends, he insisted on taking us all shopping at his expense, promising us one dress each. We were still very conscious of the state we were in but, as Conrad was able to park the car just outside the dress shop, we could slip inside with minimum exposure to the public gaze. The staff in the shop were courtesy itself. We each found a dress we liked and, with some sadness, discarded the old ones which, oil-covered as they were, were beyond resuscitation. Mine had been a cherry-coloured one, bought by my mother, of which I was particularly fond.

The next stop was a luggage shop where we were each supplied with a suitcase, after which we went on to a chemist where Conrad purchased a cake of soap, a toothbrush and a tube of toothpaste for each of us. Back at the hotel I found, waiting for me, a small parcel containing a Moffat Bible, a comb and a notebook and pencil, most welcome contributions from a missionary I had met briefly at Chan Bee's house the previous day, which now seemed so remote. The Bible was her own and was invaluable to me during the war years; I still have it.

Over the next days we learned how it was that we had come to be blown up by one of our own mines. As the story came out, it proved to be a sorry saga of human error. The Captain, who had carefully charted the position of the minefield as given to him in Rangoon, had thought no more about it except to assume that he now knew how to avoid it. Sometime between Rangoon and Singapore, a radio message had been received reporting alterations in the position of the minefield. The radio officer took the message to the bridge immediately but, not finding the Captain there at that moment, left it in what he considered to be a safe and obvious place. For some reason the Captain never saw it. The assumption was that it must have been blown away.

The pilot whose job it was to see friendly ships safely on their way out of the harbour had a date on shore that morning and was anxious to get back quickly. The Captain, having assured him that the minefield was on his chart, had given him permission to leave. He then took the course he had marked on his chart and steered straight into disaster.

A naval rating on duty on a British destroyer watched helplessly as we headed into the middle of the minefield. He was in a position to fire a warning shot across the bows of friendly vessels going the wrong way but only with the permission of his superior officer whom he could not find. He apparently did not dare to do it on his own initiative.

We were told that, as the ship swung round in crazy circles, we should have hit at least ten other mines.

Fortunately they must have been swept aside by the ship's wash. I also learned, with some cold shivers, that the sea in those parts abounded in sharks. They too would have been kept at bay by the explosion but would have soon been back. I now appreciated the officer's insistence that I should not jump into the water.

Official loss of life was put at twenty-two. The tragedy hit a Sikh family who had attended boat drill with us from the beginning and should have been in our boat. They had panicked and were in one of the boats which capsized. Their six-month old baby boy had drowned in his mother's arms. Two older children survived. It was hard to see them across the dining room in the hotel and to have no language in which to comfort them. No mention was made in our hearing of the hundreds of deck passengers we last saw crowded on the ship's stern before she went down. There was no sign of the two Chinese girls.

There was, of course, an almost immediate investigation as a result of which the Captain lost his Master's ticket. It was a tragic end to what had been such a happy ship.

CHAPTER 11

Now it was a matter of waiting until the shipping company could get us sorted out and find berths for us all on another ship. Meanwhile they gave each of us a sum of money and permission to send two cables at their expense. As it was war time, everything had to be very hush-hush and we were limited to the cryptic message, 'Safe and well.' One of my cables went to my puzzled parents who fondly imagined I had been in China for at least two months by then and the other went to an equally puzzled Ken who had already travelled the five hundred miles through war-torn countryside on two occasions hoping to meet me. Now he would be as much in the dark as he was before.

Back at home, after the war, I learned of my parents' reactions. They had been completely mystified by the cable until, two weeks later, they had seen, in one of the daily newspapers, several pictures of a British ship sinking after hitting a mine. These must have been the photographs taken by the intrepid husband of the hysterical woman in our lifeboat. We knew he had stayed on board until the last possible minute and had then managed to get aboard a raft from which he had been rescued. Somehow he had managed to keep his film dry.

Having put two and two together, my father then told me of the experience he had a fortnight earlier. He had woken suddenly in the middle of one night having just dreamed that I was walking on a plank over the open hold of a ship. He felt I was in imminent danger and did the only thing he could do — he prayed. He had not told my mother. Perhaps, after all, it was his praying rather than my own faith which had produced that extraordinary sense of peace amidst the panic on the sloping deck.

One of my possessions which had been locked so carefully away that Sunday was my passport. It was now certainly safe from hostile use but not much use to me either. I naively imagined it would be a simple matter to get a replacement from the local authorities but, once again, I had forgotten there was a war on. I was asked for proof of my British identity which, of course, I did not have. The authorities were sympathetic but would go no further than to provide me with a document which would enable me to land in China. After that I would have to apply again.

The urgent matter now for the Company was to get us off their hands as soon as possible. The Raffles Hotel was not cheap. Finally, after ten days during which we were able to get to know local friends better, see something of the surrounding countryside and enjoy Raffles' hospitality, we were put on a Dutch luxury liner on its way to America via Manila, Hong Kong and Shanghai.

It was a large ship but only luxury for one class of passenger. For the handful of us who, up until now had been travelling second class, the Company could not afford to pay the full price so we were allotted very small cabins in the part of the ship normally used to accommodate servants attached to the legitimate passengers. This was right down in the stern of the ship and we only had access to a narrow strip of deck at cabin level and a small area on the upper deck. There was no lounge as such but only a small dining saloon with wooden chairs round the tables. A cheerful steward appeared at intervals with food for us but there would be no more fatherly care such as I had enjoyed on the *Sirdhana*.

Within sight of our bit of upper deck was a handsome swimming pool which greatly cheered our somewhat

40

sunken spirits. Without thinking, on our first day out of
Singapore, we ducked under the rail separating us from
the other passengers and joined our first class friends
from the *Sirdhana* in the pool. Our frolicking was
brought swiftly to an end by an officer who told us the
swimming pool was out of bounds to us and sent us
packing back to where we belonged in spite of our
friends' protests.

Our next port of call was Manila, a bonus for those of
us who had just come aboard as the *Sirdhana* had not
been scheduled to call there. We spent a happy, sunny
day visiting the old Spanish city where we ate ice creams
in a small courtyard surrounded by vines heavy with
purple grapes. We must have been among the last
foreign visitors to see this beautiful part of the city, later
to be bombed into oblivion. It also proved to be the last
pleasant day of the journey.

CHAPTER 12

We were hardly out at sea again before the wind began to get up and the rain to pour down. The ship pitched and rolled until it became impossible to stand upright and even sitting on a chair without falling off was difficult. The chairs themselves, fortunately, as on all ships, were anchored firmly to the floor.

We hung on tight but one by one people disappeared from the dining saloon until finally only the American journalist and I were left. Neither of us felt much like eating when our friendly steward staggered down to our quarters. After depositing our food, he proceeded to go round the cabins screwing down the porthole covers. As he did so he told us, with evident relish, that we were running straight into a typhoon which, in normal times, a ship would travel five hundred miles to avoid. It might last a few hours or even a few days. This piece of information did little to improve our appetites. It was small comfort to be told that there would be a short lull in the storm as we passed through its 'eye'. He also told us that the grand piano in the first class lounge had already broken adrift and, as it hurtled across the floor, had hit a passenger, breaking several ribs. Having delivered all this cheerful information he vanished and it would be many hours before we saw him again.

My last glimpse of the outside world before the portholes were covered over was not encouraging. It looked as though we were in the middle of a blizzard. Everything was a dense white, a mixture, I supposed, of the rain splashing down and the spray flying up. The ship seemed to be wrapped in a thick blanket of moaning roar of wind, sea and rain. The engines had slowed down some time ago and now stopped altogether. As the noise outside increased so the new silence inside the ship became almost tangible and, down in our part of it we felt totally cut off from the rest of mankind.

At one point, longing for a breath of fresh air, I went to open the door leading out on to the small stern deck. It took all my strength to push against it before it was whipped out of my hand and flew open with a crash. All I could see as I looked out astern, was a solid wall of green. Seized with overwhelming nausea, I grabbed the door and forced it shut as though that would stop the great wave from engulfing us. The deafening noise which had hit me as the door flew open, now, as suddenly, subsided back again into its muffled roar as I tottered back towards my cabin, thrown from one side of the narrow passageway to the other as I went. I stopped only to call in on the Canadian girls but they were far beyond being interested in me and my troubles. Maybe, in retrospect, there is something to be said for air travel after all.

The bunk in my cabin lay transversely across the ship which was now rolling helplessly out of control, so that, lying on it, at one moment I would be standing upright, and the next would be on my head. Between each roll there was an uncertain wobble as the poor battered ship decided whether to come upright again or not. As I clung to the sides of my bunk, I knew what it was to be really frightened. In comparison, sharks apart, escape from a sinking ship in relatively calm water seemed a simple affair. Here there could be no escape. No lifeboat could possibly be launched, let alone survive, in the sort of sea I had glimpsed outside. I was so frightened that it was difficult to keep my mind clear enough even to say 'Help, Lord!' which I tried to say many times. Any self-sufficiency which I might have had before had drained away. It was with a feeling of utter helplessness that I tried to pray for all the other people on the ship who must be feeling as scared as I was, unless they were too sick to notice. 'Trust in God' at a time like that is no longer a pious platitude but requires a hard-won act of will.

I don't remember just how long the storm lasted, only that it seemed a very long time. However it must have calmed down eventually as I fell asleep. When I woke up, the heavy rolling had stopped and the ship was now pitching in a controlled orderly way. The comforting sound of the engines had returned and it was quite clear that we were actually moving forward again. Having lost both my watch and a travelling clock it was difficult to keep track of time. I managed to unscrew the porthole cover to find that it was broad daylight outside. It did not take me long to dress and get up on deck where I was met by one of the most beautiful mornings I have ever seen. There was still quite a sea running with white horses being whipped away by the wind. Scattered round us were several seagoing Chinese junks, well battened down and their sails still furled, bobbing about like so many corks, visible one moment and out of sight the next. To our left and right were the offshore islands of Hong Kong aglow in the morning sun.

CHAPTER 13

As I stood leaning on the ship's rail, a great surge of thankfulness and relief swept over me, and I felt immeasurably lighter in spirit. So arriving in Hong Kong that morning felt like a mini-resurrection. I was able to phone the London Mission as soon as we had finished docking and one of them came down to the ship to pick me up.

It was to be another day of meeting people. Among them was Dr. Katie Wu, headmistress of a girls' school, who was later to hide all the girls in a covered (empty) swimming pool while she placidly conducted a party of Japanese soldiers round the building. Her warm 'Welcome to China!' made me feel that perhaps I was where God wanted me to be after all.

In the afternoon another friend took me by ferry across the harbour, which was swarming with boats of every size and shape, to her home in Kowloon. I felt a thrill of excitement as I looked at the hills in the distance and knew I was looking at China proper.

Before I left, the Mission promised to send a telegram to Shanghai to let the Mission there know when I was due to arrive. Thus reassured I sailed off again with renewed hope and confidence.

Hong Kong at the end of November was pleasantly warm and my cotton dress, which was fortunately capable of drying overnight, was quite adequate, but as we sailed north the temperature plummeted and by the time we reached Shanghai it was already below freezing. A kindly Dutch lady recognised my urgent need for warm clothes and produced a bright green coat which she assured me she planned to throw out anyway. Although several sizes too big for me, and a colour I would never have chosen, it was very much better than nothing. She also apologetically offered me a pair of laddered lisle stockings which I thankfully accepted. Sandals were the only footwear I possessed so they had to go with me but a sun helmet seemed too much out of place on a December morning in Shanghai. I happily abandoned it.

There were only a few passengers disembarking in Shanghai and as the ship moored well down the Whangpoo river we were taken ashore by launch. I had no idea who would meet me but was confident that someone would be there as I emerged on to the famous Bund. There were people everywhere and, even in those days, the street was jammed with traffic, cars, trams, rickshaws and bicycles. I looked around but there was no sign of anyone pushing through the crowd to greet me. The longer I waited the less anyone seemed to notice I was there. It was bitterly cold. The excitement of arriving rapidly evaporated as I started to shiver. Then my eyes lighted on the joyful sight of a round-faced Chinese youth wearing a cap with 'American Express' emblazoned on it. He had spotted me and was making his way through the throng to where I was standing. His polite 'Can I help you?' were some of the most comforting words I have ever heard.

By this time it was quite clear that I was not going to be met by anyone so the youth escorted me to a nearby telephone kiosk. It was a relief to be able to talk English and to be understood and I certainly could not have managed a Chinese telephone on my own. There was no direct dialling in those days. We looked up 'London Mission' in the telephone directory but it wasn't there. I racked my brain to think of a name I had heard connected with Shanghai. I knew there was a large London Mission hospital in the city but could not remember its name. In my sureness that I would be met, I had not troubled to make a note of any names and addresses when in Hong Kong. Finally, as my new friend waited patiently by my side, the name 'Black' came into my mind. I remembered once meeting a Mr. Black and his wife on one occasion in our church at home. There was a long list of Blacks in the directory. Shanghai housed a vast number of foreigners. However, 'A. Black' rang a bell in my mind so we decided to try that one.

As yet I had no Chinese money so the youth offered to phone for me at his own expense. There was no reply. The only thing I could do was go to that address and wait for someone to come home, hoping it would be the right person. The youth hailed a passing rickshaw into which I climbed with my nearly empty suitcase. I sat waiting while he and the coolie had a long and lively conversation. He then told me that he had given the coolie instructions to take me first to the Bureau de Change where I could get some Chinese money and then on to this address we had decided on. When we arrived there I was to give him so much money and no more.

So off we set into the melee of Shanghai traffic. I never did get to the point of feeling comfortable sitting perched up in a rickshaw, tilted slightly backward and pulled along by a trotting fellow human being in tattered clothing and, more often than not, barefooted. On this occasion it all seemed too much like a dream to take seriously and I felt more like laughing than anything else at the sheer unlikeliness of it all. Here was I, still only twenty-three, a European girl alone with an unknown coolie in the middle of a city renowned for its vice and violence, yet I felt perfectly safe in his hands. And so it proved to be. He waited patiently while I changed some money, collecting a handful of rather grubby little notes, and then he padded off in the opposite direction and over what later I knew to be the Soochow Creek, until we came to a large block of modern flats in which 'A. Black' was reputed to live. I still look back with amazement at the one and only time I handed over money to a rickshaw coolie without any haggling. I didn't realise till much later what a paragon of a rickshaw coolie he was.

The plush carpeting of the foyer of Broadway Mansions was like another world. I went up by lift to the flat labelled 'Black' and the door was opened by a Chinese woman who directed me downstairs again to another flat where Mrs. Black was playing Bridge with neighbours. Mr. Black was out. When Mrs. Black came to the door of her friend's flat, she took one look at me and shut the door hurriedly behind her. I was very ready to agree I was no fit sight for her friends, but she was the right Mrs. Black. She escorted me up to her flat, made a phone call to the Mission secretary who lived on the other side of the city, then, with an apology for doing so, left me while she went back to her game of Bridge.

It was a great relief to find that the local secretary was, in fact Mr. Baxter who had stayed in our home more than once and his greeting when he arrived at the flat was warm and welcoming. Apparently the cable he should have received from Hong Kong had never arrived. Minutes later we were at his home and Mrs. Baxter, a comfortable-looking but smartly dressed lady, was opening the door for us. Words of welcome died on her lips as she looked me up and down, from the old green coat to the laddered stockings and sandals, and an expression of horror came over her face as she exclaimed, 'My dear child, what would your mother say!' I felt like a very small girl who had been lost and found as she opened her arms to embrace me and pull me in out of the cold.

First thing the next morning I was rushed to the shops to be fitted out from top to bottom with clothes suitable to the freezing temperature. These included a much smarter coat than I was used to wearing and a little pillbox hat which I never wore again. It all seemed too much of a contrast to the bodies we were passing lying in the gutters, some of whom moved a little and some who did not, frozen to death where they lay and waiting to be removed by the refuse collectors.

To my surprise I found I had landed in the middle of yet another MRA campaign. It was being run by a group of local Chinese and members of the staff of the Mission Hospital. There were colourful posters dotted around the city so I felt very much at home. I was even invited to take part in a broadcast for the local American radio station, an odd beginning to life in China.

At the end of the week I was put on board a coastal steamer bound for Tienjing and was reunited with my two large boxes which had been waiting for me for two months. It was to be an extremely cold two-day journey. The boat was completely blacked out because of the war already being waged between China and Japan. The light in my cabin was too dim to read by and there was little warmth. I spent most of the time on my bunk under the blankets. The only entertainment was meal times when I watched spellbound as men in immaculate Chinese gowns, sitting at small tables in a circle round the saloon, spat flawlessly into a large pot in the middle, placed there for the purpose but looking more as though it was waiting for an aspidistra.

At Taku Bar, the mouth of the Tienjing river, we were transferred, after spending the night in freezingly cold wooden huts, to a small steamer with reinforced

49

bows, which ploughed its fascinating way through great blocks of ice. Just as Tienjing itself came in sight, a woman, in rapid Chinese, made it clear with the aid of hand signals, that she would like me to keep an eye on her baby, which she had dumped on a seat in the saloon, while she went up on deck.

I could see the approaching quay out of the corner of my eye. Ken, if he had got the message from Shanghai, should be on it by now. What on earth would he feel if I didn't show up? Little did I know then that he had made the trip to meet me twice already. Despair began to get hold of me as the boat inched ever closer and there were no signs of the baby's mother returning. Finally, when I could stand it no longer, I abandoned the baby and shot up on deck.

There he was among the crowd on the quayside, looking just the same as he had two years ago, with maybe a little less hair on his head. In spite of not having fallen in love with him, it was extraordinarily good to see him and, as we fell into each other's arms, I felt as though I was where I truly belonged. At that moment we seemed totally isolated from the noise and the hubbub surrounding us.

CHAPTER 14

Ken had been destined to take over an eighty bed hospital in a village, Xiaochang, in the middle of the vast north China plain. He had finally arrived there in the autumn of 1938 having already spent six months in the language school in Beijing and a further six months under supervision in another mission hospital on the banks of the Grand Canal.

Xiaochang hospital served an area the size of Wales with a population of about ten million. It was forty miles from the nearest railway station. There were no roads as such. Travel was by foot, bicycle or mule cart along ruts through the fields. The journey took two or three days in normal times. By the time Ken arrived, the Japanese had already invaded China and were struggling to control the countryside. Preventing them in the north was the Chinese Communist eighth route army, locally known as the much feared 'Ba Lu', which carried on ceaseless guerrilla warfare. In addition, bandits pursued their ancient ways, waylaying travellers and relieving them of their goods and, sometimes, their lives. Travel of any kind was extremely hazardous.

In addition to the hospital, the mission boasted a large church and an excellent school. The half dozen or so missionaries working there lived in a compound surrounded by high walls just outside the village. It had been there for seventy-five years. Now the Japanese had built a mud fort a few hundred yards from the compound. The Chinese would use the far wall of our compound as cover for firing their mortar shells over our heads into the fort.

Ken now found himself busier than he had ever been, even as a junior doctor in England. There had been a

Chinese doctor in the hospital but, because of threats to his life from the Communists if he continued to work there, the Mission reluctantly let him go. Ken was saddled with all the surgical, medical and obstetrical work plus having to travel up to Tienjing to collect drugs and equipment, since it was safer for him to make the journey than for the Chinese. He was also responsible for paying the staff, but this had to be done in currency approved by the Communists which had to be collected secretly in Tienjing and smuggled back through the Japanese lines.

Fortunately Ken was helped by a highly efficient Scottish matron and her well-trained staff of Chinese nurses who, with considerable courage, cheerfully stuck to their jobs. After a few months, Eric Liddell, the Olympic gold medallist and hero of the film *Chariots of fire*, who was teaching in Tienjing, was sent down, at his own request, to help out. As well as working as an evangelist, he took much of the business side of running the hospital off Ken's shoulders, in addition living in Ken's house and giving much needed moral support.

Eric too, had met the Oxford Group in Scotland and had become totally convinced that 'When man listens, God speaks'. This was to prove a matter of life and death for both of them in the dangerous days that lay ahead, depending on God to tell them precisely what to do and when to do it. They would often get a message to go to a village where help was needed and on one of these occasions as they cycled over a field all seemed peaceful. Ken was riding ahead of Eric when he had the sudden thought, 'jump off'. As they did so, a hailstorm of bullets flew over their heads.

On one of these trips Ken was picked up by a group of Communist soldiers who took him in for questioning.

Setting up a mock trial, they condemned him to death. He pointed out that if they killed him they would lose the help of the hospital on which they depended so heavily for the treatment of their own casualties. They released him. Others were less fortunate. Several Roman Catholic priests working in an adjoining area were murdered. It had been no idle threat.

Thinking of the need for self protection from soldiers, bandits and the like, someone offered Ken a beautiful little pistol. He fell for it in a big way and showed it to Eric. Eric reacted by warning him to have nothing to do with it. 'If you meet trouble', he said, 'you will find yourself depending on your gun instead of God — don't touch it!'

Ken often slept in the hospital, as crossing the open space between it and the mission compound after dark was too dangerous. Night was the time when the Chinese army moved around, tearing down telephone wires and digging up ground which the Japanese would need to travel along. The trigger-happy Japanese soldiers would shoot at any moving shadow at these times without troubling to find out who it belonged to.

On one of these nights, Ken was woken by something cold pressing against his forehead. Out of the darkness came a voice demanding that its owner be taken immediately to a certain patient. This patient had been brought in with both arms and legs broken after jumping down a well to avoid capture. Apparently he was a Japanese spy. Ken refused and insisted that no patient was known by name or occupation. Anyone needing treatment was treated without question.

Finally he was left, still with a gun at his head, while the rest of the gang rampaged through the hospital until they found their victim, easily identifiable because of his injuries. Japanese spies were also easily identified by the hard skin between their first two toes caused by the sandals they wore when not disguised as a Chinese. The gun was withdrawn from Ken's head and there was silence. A few moments later Ken heard several shots being fired outside the hospital after which all the guns in the Japanese fort opened up. Early the next morning the patient's body was found on open ground lying on a hospital blanket.

The question now was, how would the Japanese react? Ken hurried back to his house to rouse Eric. Together they were quiet and asked God what they should do. The thought came clearly that Ken should go by himself, wearing a white coat, to the Japanese as soon as possible and give his version of the night's events before anyone else could give theirs. No one shot at him as he crossed over to the nearby fort. It took a while for the guard to understand that he wanted to see 'Number One' but eventually he was let in and taken to an inner room which was full of soldiers. On a bed, with his back to Ken, lay the commanding officer. He barked an order and the room emptied. Then he rolled over towards Ken and, with a broad grin said, in faultless American, 'Forget it, Buddy!'

There then followed a long conversation in which the Commander admitted to hating his job as a soldier. 'You heal people, I kill them,' he said. He had grown up in California and his mother was a Christian. Shortly after this incident he disappeared and was replaced by one with less refined feelings.

CHAPTER 15

Before he made one of his journeys to Tienjing, to collect drugs and supplies, a group of parents from the village came begging Ken to take their children with him. They were due to start at the middle school in Techow, the town on the railway. They had started out on their journey but had been turned back by one or other of the warring groups. They felt Ken would have a better chance of getting them through.

On a September morning they set off, twenty children and their belongings stacked on wheelbarrows the wheels of which always squeaked to keep evil spirits at bay. The squeak did little to deter other predators. It was hard enough pushing their way along the ruts through the fields but, to add to the difficulties, there was still a lot of flood water around and parts of the journey had to be by boat. As they were crossing from one village to the next, a gun battle broke out over their heads. However, they crossed safely and looked for somewhere to spend the night. The inn was full but a farmer offered them his pigsty. The children bedded down in the straw and Ken lay across the entrance to protect them. They agreed to set out again when the first cock crowed.

As soon as Ken heard the cock he roused the children, all very unwilling to be woken up. It was still dark as they stumbled along, the wheelbarrows constantly tipping over into ditches and finally being abandoned, each child carrying its own belongings. As the dawn failed to appear, Ken began to realise he must have dreamed up the cock and had got them all away far too early. He was very apologetic. The rest of the journey was uneventful, apart from Ken having to carry some of the smaller children over floodwater, and they were safely deposited in their new school.

On his return journey Ken arrived at the village where they had spent the night, to find it a burnt-out ruin with only a few old women searching through the rubble for any belongings which could be salvaged. They told Ken that, well before dawn that morning, the Japanese had raided the village, which was suspected of sheltering guerrilla soldiers. They had confiscated every cart and animal, taking off every able-bodied inhabitant before setting fire to their homes.

On the North China plain one was seldom out of sight of a village. One of these Ken planned to visit as he was trudging home one day across the fields. Just as he was about to turn towards the one on his left, he heard someone telling him he should go instead to the one on his right. He found the people there in a state of great excitement. They told him that the other village had just been occupied by the Japanese. Their own village had a number of wounded 'Ba Lu' soldiers needing his attention. How had he known to come to them? Ken replied that a man in the field had told him to. When they looked out across the fields there was no one to be seen and then Ken realised that the 'man' had spoken to him in English — he was no Chinese farmer!

One of the soldiers had a gunshot wound through the thigh which had fractured his femur and Ken arranged for him to be brought into hospital. As he was recovering he owned up to having shot himself in order to be admitted to the hospital where he hoped to hear more about 'your Jesus'. He had overheard Ken being questioned on one occasion and could think of no other way to find out more. Like the Japanese commander, he too was sickened of fighting and killing. In hospital he became a Christian and, on his recovery, the Mission sent him away to Tienjing to be trained as a teacher.

News came one day of a wounded Chinese soldier who was being hidden in a nearby village. Eric set out with the hospital cart to bring him into hospital. The man had been with a group of Communist soldiers who had been ambushed by the Japanese. They had been made to dig their own graves after which they were beheaded. This one, a tall man had refused to kneel down. The Japanese soldier had taken a swipe at his neck whereupon he had fallen into the 'grave' and been left for dead. The villagers found him alive when they came out to search the bodies for anything of value and had hidden him behind a decrepit idol in their tumble-down temple. His jaw bone had saved him. Ken operated as best he could and slowly the man recovered.

One morning, the man called Ken over to his bedside and, speaking excellent English, told how, as he was returning home from the Peking College of Fine Art of which he was a graduate, he was caught by the Communists and forced into their service. As he refused to carry a gun, they made him their secretary.

While in hospital he had watched with great interest all that went on and the way people cared and said he would like to become a Christian. There was one great problem. However skilful the surgery, nothing could hide the ugly scar which stretched from the back of his neck to his left jaw. He was terrified that if any Communist saw it he would be dragged back into their ranks and if the Japanese saw it, he would be shot. It was decided, again after consultation with Eric, that as soon as he was well enough to be moved, he should be smuggled after dark to a neighbouring village to stay under cover with a known Christian there. When the incident had been forgotten, he would return and live in

Ken's house until he felt it safe enough to carry on with his journey home. He turned out to be a very fine painter of birds and flowers and taught Ken the secrets of Chinese painting which he uses to this day.

He was still there when I arrived and he became my most patient Chinese teacher. He took on the name of Li Shin Sheng, 'New Born', with the promise that he would tell us his real name when we finally parted company. We never did hear what it was.

CHAPTER 16

I learned from Ken that it was the way of Japanese soldiers when examining one's baggage to turn it upside down for easier viewing of the contents. I was to experience this several times. However, as we waited on the quayside at Tienjing for the inevitable to happen, we heard a voice with an American accent say, 'What are you doing here, Dr McAll?' and, looking round, were met by the smiling face of a Japanese Customs Officer. He and Ken greeted each other like long lost friends and I was introduced. He was none other than the garrison Commander of Xiaochang days. He promptly drew a large chalk 'X' on my luggage, which remained unopened, and asked us to meet him after dark in a certain restaurant where he would tell us his story.

Thus it was that, on my first evening in China proper, I was faced with the results of my Calcutta decision. The Mission had laid on a welcome for me including a prayer meeting. To turn my back on this and spend the evening fraternising with the enemy would not be popular. It seemed to me that nothing could be more important, from God's point of view, than to spend time with this man. However, I doubt whether, without Ken, who had a light-hearted disregard for what others thought, especially if any sort of adventure beckoned, I would have had the courage to do it. The displeasure was very apparent when we announced our plan. I hope we were forgiven eventually, but I'm not sure.

We duly met our friend, now in Chinese clothes, in a dimly lit cafe and he told us how he had heard of the need for an English-speaking Customs officer and had jumped at the opportunity. 'So no more killing,' he said with a smile. It seemed a strange way to start my missionary work in China and God had many more such surprises up His sleeve as we were to discover. National identities do not appear to figure very large in His sight.

My statutory six months at the language school in Beijing was now the next item on the agenda. Once that was over we would be free to get married. Still having no doubts that this was what God wanted, Ken took me off to a French jeweller's shop where he, not renowned for throwing money around, bought a highly expensive and beautiful solitaire diamond ring which flashed all the colours of the rainbow. We liked to think that the diamond stood for God's guidance which we were certainly going to need in the days ahead.

So Ken returned to Xiaochang for what were to be some of the most exciting months of his life, while I revelled in exploring the glories of Beijing, making many new friends especially among the students from Yenching University. Many of these were part of the MRA team there, so we had much in common.

As the time drew near for the wedding, Ken came up to join me in going to the British Consul to make the necessary arrangements. He would need to perform the legal part of the marriage. We had been invited to spend our honeymoon in Japan with a Japanese family we had known well in England, and for this I needed to get a new passport. The one issued in Singapore had only taken me as far as Shanghai. It seemed quite straightforward. However, things were not that simple. The Consul looked solemnly at me and said, 'How do I know you are a British citizen? What evidence do you have?' I had none, having long ago thrown away my expired driving licence. For a few icy moments I felt what it must be like to be stateless. It was like, I remembered, being kept outside the family sitting-room door until I was good enough to be allowed in again.

Quite apart from my need for a passport, wartime instructions had come from the British government forbidding the marriage of a British subject to an alien. If I couldn't prove my Britishness, the wedding was off. Finally the Consul agreed to accept a written statement from the senior member of our Mission in North China, so, having recovered from the shock, I was duly provided both with a new passport and permission to marry Ken.

On a brilliant June day in 1940 we were married, first, officially, at the rather cool, paternal hands of the Consul and later in the day by an old family friend in the packed community church. The American organist thought that the entrance of the bridegroom and best man heralded the arrival of the bride. She had played the wedding march through three times by the time the taxi, having weaved its way through the Beijing traffic, arrived, carrying me and my stand-in father. I, knowing nothing of this, could only feel excitingly welcomed by the strains of 'Here comes the Bride' and very impressed by the sight of Ken, in a smart, gleaming white, linen suit and a Macdonald tie, waiting for me at the front of the church. I was wearing the only available white dress in Beijing at that time, not quite what I would have chosen, and the same Russian lady from whom I bought it on the third floor of the Beijing hotel had provided a pretty green one for my American bridesmaid. The only available flowers were rather stiff gladioli and we spent an inordinate amount on four gardenias to put in my hair. By the end of the reception they had passed out in the heat.

But it was a joyous time under the weeping willow in the churchyard and we counted eleven different nationalities among our guests including German and French,

Chinese and Japanese: this in the middle of a war. A large proportion of them were the students. We felt greatly blessed and yet, as we drove away holding sweaty hands in the back of a taxi, I found myself thinking, 'Suppose it doesn't work? Suppose it wasn't right after all?' I had hardly finished thinking this before another thought came into my head — 'Change is always possible.' As I write this in the '90s, that might mean, 'You can always try another partner if this one's no good.' To me at that time it meant — as it still does today — that, by God's grace, if things were difficult, neither of us need go on being or doing the thing that was causing the problem. That thought proved to be the underpinning of our marriage. It never failed to be true.

Then followed an exotic two weeks in Japan, part of which was spent in a four hundred year old farmhouse equipped with all mod cons but with all the ancient farm implements still in place. It was not all holiday, though. Our host, Takasumi Mitsui, invited some of his friends to meet us. These included a high-up government minister who questioned Ken closely about the situation in China. The Japanese military were holding the reins very tightly in their hands and making it impossible for the government to get any accurate information in spite of their sending senior representatives over to find out. The last one to try was a member of the Japanese royal family who was assassinated in Beijing, officially by a Chinese but, as we learned from a reliable source later, under very suspicious circumstances. He also warned us of the likely entry of Japan into World War II and predicted the date very accurately, as we were to discover. Two weeks after we had been there, the government resigned and the military took over. As we were leaving Japan a smiling uniformed official gave us an accurate detail-by-detail

62

account of all the places we had visited while in the country. As Britishers we were even then under suspicion.

Back from Japan we revelled in a further two weeks with our fellow missionaries, sunning ourselves and swimming in the warm sea of the famous resort of Peitaiho. Here Ken introduced me to his canoe which he had made the previous summer. So, once again, like climbing terrifyingly tall beech trees as a student with Ken in Auchendinny Woods in order to be allowed my Mars Bar, I meekly accepted the challenge of the canoe as we paddled out beyond Rocky Point on a very rough day, the fragile bamboo craft creaking and bending with every wave and coming in to land behind enormous breakers which completely obscured the beach. I was to learn that, with Ken, I was likely to survive even if we didn't always deserve to.

CHAPTER 17

Neither the Japanese who controlled the area by day nor the Chinese Communists who controlled it by night appreciated the presence of the Mission, the Japanese because we represented western influence and might well be spies and the Communists because we were Christians. The Mission was very much part of the local scene, all the local children attending the school and the large church full every Sunday.

Another English-speaking Commander was appointed to the Japanese garrison with the specific task of getting us out. He told us he disliked the job he had been given but nevertheless carried it out with great efficiency, issuing demands which made the daily functioning of the Mission, especially the hospital, impossible.

The Chinese Communists opened their own school and forced all the children to attend with threats of trouble in the future if they did not. It became increasingly dangerous for any Chinese to be associated with us. We learned later that, as soon as we had left and the Japanese had pulled out, they demolished all the buildings — houses, church, school and hospital, to wipe out any memory of us.

On a bitter January day in 1941 we abandoned our homes and our work, carrying what we could on mule carts across the frozen rutted fields to the railway, two days' journey away. I was three months pregnant.

Ken and I were invited to become medical officers to the university, staff and students, in Japanese-occupied Shantung province, where Ken's father had done his translating work. His desk was still as he had left it. Ken was responsible for the men and I for the women. It was a job we could happily have done for life.

But the threat of Japan joining forces with Germany became ever more apparent and in May 1941 plans were made for the repatriation of American and British women and children. Many jumped at the opportunity to get out while the going was good.

Next door to us on the campus lived another doctor, Godfrey Gale, and his Canadian wife, Betty. Betty was expecting her first baby at almost exactly the same time as I was. Both our husbands were prepared for us to go and left it to us to decide. I could not believe that God, who had seemed so determined to get us married, should wish us to separate so soon with all the uncertainties ahead, the differing experiences we might go through and the difficulties of getting together again. I decided to stay. Betty courageously packed and unpacked three times but finally reached the same conclusion. It was a decision neither of us was ever to regret.

The babies duly arrived in July, Betty's Margaret, ten very long days before my Elizabeth. Life for all of us, including the students who frequented our homes, took on a new dimension. Our homes were more popular than ever.

Some of the students had been working with us on a plan for a time of morning prayer, following a pattern Ken and I had found useful. This was to be printed on a card, English on one side and Chinese on the other. We met, with a strange sense of urgency, on Saturday morning, December 6th, 1941, feeling that the card ought to be ready and distributed the next day. Three of the students, one of whom understood and was given permission to use the University printing press, worked until after midnight to get it done. On Sunday the cards were handed out to all the students. On Monday morning we heard that Pearl Harbour had been bombed by the

Japanese. By the end of Monday, every Chinese, apart from one or two gallant servants who opted to stay with us, had left, and Japanese soldiers patrolled every corner of the campus with us shut inside. It became our first internment camp and marked the end of our short missionary career.

More details of our years in China and especially of our time of internment have already been written up in the book, *The Moon Looks Down,* and I have been asked repeatedly over the years to retell the old story, perhaps because it was a profound learning time which has stayed with us.

However that may be, we were for nearly four years shut up in four different camps with a mixture of any human beings who could claim British, American or Dutch nationality. They came from every walk of life — business people, University professors, a Bishop, a couple of ex-Sing Sing convicts, the black crew of a scuttled American liner, ships' engineers and missionaries of various denominations. It was a medley of rich and poor now reduced to an enforced equality. The Gales and ourselves had decided to stay together, if possible, for the sake of the two children and mutual support.

In our first specially set up camp, a deserted mission school in a city on the Grand Canal, we were the doctors for three hundred people and younger than most. Having worked in the Chinese countryside, we reckoned we knew more than Shanghai dwellers about the risks of dirty water, absence of sanitation, pests and inadequate food. We very soon began to lay down the law about the precautions people should take, such as the importance of using mosquito nets, swatting flies and eating potato skins — when available. Ken even drew funny pictures illustrating the points he was trying to make.

To our surprise no one seemed to appreciate our efforts and there was open rebellion. People who had been turned out of their luxury city apartments, deprived of their freedom and used to paying for the services of their pin-striped trousered personal physicians, were not going to be pushed around by 'bloody young missionaries' as we found ourselves being called. To demonstrate the strength of their feelings, the cooks, one day, served up the midday meal of vegetable stew with the usual bits of pig fat and bristles floating in it, without having washed the mud off the vegetables, thereby making it uneatable and, with some strange process of reasoning managing to blame the doctors.

Our reputation was fortunately salvaged by a teenage youth springing an acute appendicitis. As no proper hospital facilities had as yet been set up for our use, we had to turn to and operate with one pair of artery forceps, one scalpel, one pair of rubber gloves and a very small bottle of chloroform between us. With the whole camp then rallying round to support us, help provide hot water and clean out a room, the operation went ahead and the youth made an uninterrupted recovery. We were truly grateful and had learned a salutary lesson.

Quite apart from the ever present threat of our Japanese captors, uncertainty about the future and the general unpleasantness of our position, one of the hardest things to take had been the interruption of the work which we had felt was supposed to be ours. So it was with a great lift to my spirit, as we walked through the large iron gates of our next 'home', to be given the thought 'This is the next bit of life. Get on and live it.' Apparently from God's point of view it mattered little where we were or who we were with. He would be there anyway and everyone, whatever their nationality, was important to Him.

It was a large redbrick condemned warehouse in an area opposite Shanghai which had been heavily bombed by the Japanese in 1937. Most of the windows were patched up with paper. The place had been used as a coal dump for years. Sixteen rooms, twenty foot high, housed 1200 inmates. We occupied a 13 x 9 ft corner of one of these with Godfrey and Betty and our two small girls. Half of this space was the boarded-over shaft, including the oily cables, of an elevator which had been pulled up to the next floor where it made a room for another family.

Four hundred of us had been transferred from up-country including two hundred females. As it had been a males-only camp until then, we caused quite a flutter. It was not considered suitable for families but we had been 'asked' to go there as there was a shortage of doctors.

We soon discovered the set-up was anything but happy. A gang of internees, self-appointed 'police', seemed to be in control of the internal running of the camp including the kitchen. Theft and bribery were rife, the kitchens were filthy, food was not being fairly distributed and there was scant attention to public health. People kept themselves to themselves, sitting tight on their precious belongings in their own corners. As long as we obeyed their rules and did not offend them in any way — not an easy thing to avoid, our Japanese captors left us pretty much to our own devices.

CHAPTER 18

The lesson from our previous camp had been well learned and, although it was clear that much needed to change, we left well alone waiting for God to show his hand. This He did, as usual, in an unexpected way.

The only place in the camp where it was possible to have a private conversation was the small area adjoining the eight-bed mixed-ward hospital. Here the doctors, three of them, held their daily surgeries. As is usual with all general practices, patients often came with a thin veneer of physical complaints covering up the true underlying personal problems and in the camp there were plenty of these.

One of the first to consult Ken was Fred, a Shanghai bank manager. His wife had been evacuated to Australia leaving him not only alone and suffering the indignities of internment but also deeply unhappy as they had parted on a sour note and he had no way of putting this right. He found Ken a ready listener and felt greatly relieved of his burden.

Shortly afterwards, he developed bronchitis which turned into a life-threatening broncho-pneumonia. We had no drugs with which to treat him and feared the worst. He had become a close friend.

Late one evening, sure that he was dying, he sent for Ken and asked him to pray for his wife and daughter whom he did not expect to see again. He did not ask prayers for himself. Needless to say we had all been praying. The next day Ken met him walking around apparently fully recovered. It was the first time we had witnessed such a healing. In his gratitude for what had happened, Fred offered to help the doctors in any way he could. Ken suggested they should get together each morning to think and pray about the camp situation. Very soon other ex-patients and Godfrey joined them. They met secretly in a store-room under the stairs, since meetings, apart from very visible ones in the room set aside as a common-room, were strictly forbidden. Betty and I stayed upstairs with the children as it was considered too dangerous for either of us to join in.

The time, early in the morning, was spent discussing the current problems, then being quiet to allow God to put His thoughts into their minds. These thoughts proved to be intensely practical, the first one being to create an alternative 'police' force raised from men who were large in physique and spirit. The plan was carried out with the utmost secrecy. Even Betty and I had no idea of it.

One morning, when we were all trooping out for our morning roll-call to the playing-field created out of the bombed village, there was a stalwart male at every vantage point round the building and by the laundry troughs, his hands behind his back, legs apart and a red armband with 'Police' sewn on loudly in black.

They had been prepared for open conflict with the 'gang' but nothing happened: even their so-called office, which had turned into a brothel, was abandoned without question. They vanished like rats into a hole. The Japanese took no notice.

The result was beyond all expectations. There was a sudden release of tension right through the camp and with it an almost immediate sense of community. Individuals began to offer what talents they had for the benefit of anyone wanting to make use of them. Classes started up in a wide variety of subjects. We possessed in our midst all the necessary expertise. People found talents they hadn't known they had for acting or singing. Women were suddenly willing to dig out precious articles of clothing to be used in drama presentations. A former military band conductor turned a small group of jazz musicians plus a few other instrumentalists, including me on a borrowed violin, into a symphony orchestra producing a concert once a month with music apparently appearing from nowhere to be skilfully orchestrated for this medley bunch of instruments. What did not appear was even more skilfully written out from memory. Fred started up a library: books, which had been carefully kept out of sight, poured in for anyone to borrow.

Unknown to anyone else, the early morning group went on meeting. They managed to initiate democracy in the camp, each room having its own captain who sat on a camp committee. This gave us, for the first time, more official access to the Commandant. Ken, using his artistic skills, thought up subjects for cartoon paintings, aimed at holding a mirror to ourselves and our — not always helpful — attitudes. These went up on a notice board in the common-room past which everyone had to queue for their meals. He used a Chinese brush and ink on good absorbent paper provided by the Emperor for quite another purpose. It was a sacrifice well worth making.

As time went by food became less and less, only white cabbage and rat-infested rice lasting out. American air-raids became more frequent and we had no hiding place. In summer, bedbugs thrived on our thinning blood. Our clothes rotted with sweat. In winter we froze, the temperature dropping to -10C. There was no heating and much of the inmates' clothing had vanished en route between camps. Ken and I shared one and a half pairs of winter pyjamas. The Japanese became more and more jittery and therefore even less kindly disposed towards us. It was clear that they were suffering terrible losses,

71

though no concrete news came our way.

It was on such a morning that, for the only time in four years, I doubted my decision to refuse repatriation and stay with Ken. I had dressed Elizabeth in all the clothes available including a navy blue serge outfit with a hood, made by one of the camp ladies. But she sat shrivelled up. Her white, peaky face and her thin little figure tied knots round my heart and nothing I could do would entice her to move or smile. For a moment I even doubted God.

As I hugged her, trying to get some warmth into her, I remembered again my first experience of His love in the dark days of my teenage years and as she slowly recovered, my doubts faded. I got out the smiling photo of East London Annie and hope was restored.

And the spirit of the camp survived; so much so that, at our last Christmas in 1944, in spite of the cold, the uncertainty about our future and no turkey or presents, we had to hold two services to accommodate everyone and several people said it was the best Christmas they had ever had. One lady, with tears running down her cheeks, said it was the first time she had understood what Christmas was all about.

The day finally came when the Japanese, deprived now of their clattering ancestral swords, marched out of the camp, their humiliating duties over. We were free to leave. We tottered out of the iron gate feeling as though we had just got up after a bad attack of flu. Godfrey, unknown to us at that time, had TB. I was grossly anaemic. All four adults had also lost about four stone in weight. Elizabeth, now four, was the weight of a two year old, but miraculously we had all survived, including, most marvellously, the children.

72

CHAPTER 19

For the weeks we had to wait before a ship came to take us home, we were invited to stay in an American Mission compound run by a fellow ex-internee. The authorities gave us each a million Chinese dollars, the only time any of us was likely to be a millionaire. But the excitement did not last long. An egg cost $2000 and a loaf of bread $5000. Elizabeth was in need of shoes, having been wearing for far too long a pair made by Ken from an adult shoe kindly donated by a lady in camp. Her first new pair of plimsolls cost $250,000 and a much-needed dress half a million. We were paupers again in no time.

A local Chinese family entertained us to a sumptuous twenty-dish Chinese meal which Ken's stomach felt too shrunken to take. Mine had no such problem. For Elizabeth these were days of discovery. She was alarmed by trees waving over her head and, when I lifted her up to look over a wall into a barn where a herd of cows was being milked, she almost jumped out of my arms with shock. The only cows she had seen so far were on picture postcards and she expected them all to be that size.

We were among the first to be taken off on a converted cargo ship which had been the first vessel to land troops in Normandy on D-Day. For this she had been awarded a silver bugle and each morning we were woken by its silvery sound. I had been given liver injections to be administered on the journey but caused great embarrassment in the sick bay when I presented myself. I was the first female the poor orderly had had to deal with and it was with a very red face that he stuck the needle into the appropriate place.

It was not the most comfortable of journeys. Betty

and I with the children were best off sharing what had been an officer's cabin with other mothers and children. Ken had to bed down in the hold between the ribs of the ship. Several ladders had to be climbed to reach fresh air. As the sea was rough most of the time, no one was particularly interested in food and not everyone reached the deck in time. However, ten days in Colombo waiting for a larger ship revived us. Ken was housed in an Air Force camp and women and children in a hospital where we were given, amongst other delights, milk and bananas.

Any woman who had only one dress was allowed to choose one off the rack at the local Red Cross centre. While waiting in a long queue, I spotted a dress I liked. Once again I was on the receiving end of charity but very choosy. I could almost have attacked any female getting to the rack before me and taking that dress. Happily, for them and me, no one did. Elizabeth meanwhile had been swept away by a charming Red Cross nurse and reappeared, wrapped in a large bath towel and smelling sweetly of talcum powder. The nurse begged me to let her find a dress for her as she could not bear to put the old one back on again.

Our arrival home was a highly emotional affair. We had had no news from home for over a year and did not even know if there would be anyone there to meet us. But there on the dockside were my parents and younger sister. My father's hair was now white instead of the burnished gold I had last seen it. Unknown to us, my sister had been married for nearly a year and Ken's much loved aunt who had helped to look after them all throughout their childhood had died. Several people we had known well, including a cousin and the boy across the road, had been killed or were missing.

Southampton, where we landed off a Union Castle liner converted to a troopship, had great flattened areas with weeds growing in them. The piers off Bournemouth beach, deliberately wrecked to avoid the Germans using them, stood rusty and forsaken. Familiar iron railings were missing.

The atmosphere was different too, though this was hard to pinpoint. There was something less relaxed about it. 'British Made' no longer seemed to stand for the absolute guarantee of quality it once had done. One even had to insure luggage or a bicycle before sending them by train, something I had never dreamed of doing during my years of going backwards and forwards from Edinburgh as a student.

And yet the same sopranos in the choir at our old church were still opening their mouths and hurling their voices at the altos opposite as though nothing had changed and it was difficult to imagine what they had been through in the intervening years, just as it was for them, or even our own families, to understand us. A large gap in experience had opened up between us and it could never be closed completely.

Being a long way away and shut up in an internment camp had greatly heightened our memories of home. During those years I had often, along with delicious dreams of roast lamb, peas and crisp brown potatoes, dreamed of my mother walking in through the camp gate and being hugged by her as only she could hug. She, along with Britain itself, had seemed the epitome of all that was loving, warm, safe and trustworthy.

Not only did I find myself disillusioned with Britain but sadly also with my beloved mother. Elizabeth, now four and a half, was the first of their five grandchildren my parents had seen, my two elder sisters also having been overseas right through the war. Fairly naturally she was the centre of attention.

Although we had tried to bring her up in as civilised a manner as possible under the circumstances, Elizabeth's behaviour clearly left much to be desired in the eyes of her grandmother, and Ken and I both found ourselves feeling irritated by her constant correcting of her. Fortunately for all of us we had learned the value, and the possibility, of bringing our feelings into the open rather than letting them ferment and grow. The rift was soon healed and closeness re-established.

I was now pregnant again. Ken and I had carefully avoided any chance of this happening until, in the closing weeks of internment, when the likelihood of our survival was at its slimmest, we suddenly felt we were being told to go ahead with having a family. It was like a red light turning green and our first promise of peace.

In spite of severe malnutrition it had happened and within weeks we had been literally bombarded with food from the skies dropped by American bombers which seemed to know exactly where we were. On the way home I and another pregnant woman were treated with great care and generosity and for six weeks after getting home all of us were allowed double rations of meat, milk, sugar and butter. My mother said later that we had looked like skeletons when we walked off the ship.

Having stayed some weeks with my parents recuperating, we felt it only right to spend some time with Ken's mother and sisters in Edinburgh. We took it for granted that they would regard this as a great blessing. Now that I am the age Ken's mother was then, I realise what an imposition it was. The house was a small one. My mother-in-law had to move out of her comfortable good-sized bedroom into a small back room to make room for us. On still meagre rations and small income, we had to be fed. Small wonder if Granny occasionally had words over the table with our hungry daughter as she tucked voraciously into the jam and other previously unknown delights of home food. I would haul a howling bundle upstairs until things quietened down, then return to the table to see who could be the first to make Granny laugh.

CHAPTER 20

Ken escaped much of this. He was hardly ever at home. In no time he was being asked by friends to exhibit his war-time drawings and over the next few months he held fifteen exhibitions in various galleries around the country. He also tried his hand at commercial art and was given one or two small commissions. This whetted his appetite for more. For a time he considered quitting medicine altogether and after an exciting visit to Alexandra Palace rather fancied getting into the cartoon-film world. It was a heady dream.

One of our friends, Ernest Claxton, a secretary with the British Medical Association, had taken on the job of fighting the idea, then being proposed, of a government salaried service for doctors if and when a National Health Service ever came into being. Memories of the way German doctors had been manipulated by the Nazis were still only too fresh in many people's minds. It was of great importance to keep doctors' clinical freedom intact. Ernest asked Ken if he would draw cartoons for a film-strip to be used around the country as propaganda.

The point was won and, when the NHS did materialise, family doctors went into it on a contract basis so that they could, theoretically at least, opt out of the service if they felt threatened by government pressure at any time. This remains the official basis of their employment though opting out has become virtually impossible.

Christmas came. Though I much enjoyed being with my mother and sisters-in-law, Ken's younger sister was still working as a nurse in Edinburgh at that time, and meeting up with many old friends, I was very homesick for my own parents and longed for the baby to arrive.

Having booked up with a doctor and a nursing home I needed to stay put till it did.

In early March we were offered the use of a friend's house in Kingussie on Speyside for two weeks. This was just what we were needing. The hills were covered with snow as deep as the heather it covered. As the baby was due at the end of the month, the first thing we did was to notify the local midwife of our presence in the area. Then we settled down to enjoy the first chance of being on our own as a family which we had had in nearly five years.

The house boasted an Aga, warm and available at any time. We would put a saucepan of oats on it overnight ready for breakfast, after which we would sally forth into the crisp March air rejoicing in our freedom to scramble over the hills. Elizabeth became very protective of me with my load and with great care helped me over humps of heather and little streams. We kept ourselves going on the luxuries of apples and chocolate but, in spite of being piggybacked by Ken for much of the way, Elizabeth's stamina failed as the day wore on and a sad little refrain started up, 'I'm cold and tired and hungry', to be oft repeated in the family as the years went by. Returning to a warm house and yet another large bowl of porridge, she soon recovered. At the end of this treatment we felt truly recuperated and rejoiced to see Elizabeth beginning to fill out and her cheeks becoming pink.

Then it was back to Edinburgh. I was invited out to tea to meet a highly respectable lady. She asked politely when the baby was due. When I said, 'Tomorrow', she turned deathly pale and quickly changed the subject. I think she expected it to arrive there and then.

Two days later, on April 1st, it did arrive. No one ever forgets Jean's birthday and, although Ken and I can both boast of having good Scottish blood in our veins, she reckons she is one up on the rest of the family because of having actually been born in Scotland.

Her arrival, apart from the fact that she screamed for two hours every evening for the first two or three weeks, proved a great asset in the peace-keeping process. If Granny was upset over our behaviour, as she had every right to be, we only had to drop Jean in her arms for her to start purring like a contented pussy cat. It was a joy to see them together.

CHAPTER 21

With Jean two months old we relieved Ken's family of our presence and set off back to my home in Bournemouth. Missing the evening connection at Waterloo station meant waiting for two hours for the slow tenthirty train to Bournemouth, reminiscent of some of our China journeys, only this time there were seats to sit on. I fed Jean in the dim privacy of the Ladies' waiting room.

We finally arrived home in the early hours. My sister Margie had arrived from America with John and their two children a few days earlier. They had had to flee from Burma when the Japanese moved in and had spent the war partly in India and later in America. Rachel, their eldest, was just six months older than Elizabeth who was to occupy a bed next to her in a room on the top floor. We all, grandparents as well, crept up as quietly as we could but the excitement had been too much. Rachel was wide awake. She and Elizabeth who, apart from Margie her wartime companion, had never met anyone of her own size at close quarters before, sat on their beds and stared at each other in complete silence for several moments. Then they started to giggle uncontrollably and the laughing spread to the adults till we were all shedding tears of sheer delight at being together.

All over the country, families were being reunited. By Christmas 1946 our eldest sister Catherine arrived back with Burford and their three children. Burford had served as a medical officer with the Indian army. Our youngest sister, now a fully competent physiotherapist and the only one to have been in Britain throughout the war, joined us. In the drawing room was a Christmas tree reaching to the ceiling.

In the afternoon of Christmas Day, Jean, now eight months and old enough to take a lively interest in the proceedings, was christened in front of the tree by John and Burford's father, a Congregational minister, out of a bowl used at her grandfather's christening. The bowl had also been used at the christenings of several other members of his large family.

Christmas over, we had to get down to the serious business of our future and the need to earn our living. We had nothing coming in and the Mission had not been able to pay us anything for our years in internment. Apart from a few savings, we were at this moment dependent on my parents for food and lodging. They were about to pack up and abandon the old home to move across the bay to Swanage to another old family home built by my grandfather as a summer residence for the family. He apparently had thought nothing of moving the whole household, servants and all, every six months, in the days of horse-drawn transport. He would go every day to his office in the rapidly growing town of Bournemouth by paddle steamer. My father and his brothers went to school the same way.

Fortunately for us, my father had earlier bought up the house next door which had been roughly converted into flats. He offered us the ground floor flat, now conveniently vacant, with a modest interest-free loan to be repaid over the next few years. We had no furniture of our own and no money to buy it with, but this obstacle was easily overcome by removing a few planks from the fence between the two houses and shoving through all the old furniture which my parents no longer wanted. No removal vans were needed. It may not have been the most beautiful or modern of furniture but it provided beds to sleep on, chairs to sit on and oversized wardrobes to hang our few clothes in. Most of these things we still possess and use.

The next urgent question was what should we do? We had resigned from the Mission knowing that China was closed to us. We might have been offered alternative work in India or Africa but we had no feeling that God wanted us to go just anywhere. Ken's venture into commercial art had not shown much promise for the future.

Two friends, one a doctor, came to visit us. The doctor said, 'Think of the most needy member of the family and you will find the right plan'. It was obvious, as we sat quietly, listening for God's thoughts, that Elizabeth was the one whose needs were greatest — more important than our careers. She badly needed a settled home.

'Why don't you put up a plate at your gate and start a general practice?' asked the doctor. It was still possible to do that in those pre-NHS days without asking anyone's permission but it could be risky. Bournemouth was already a popular place for doctors. However, it felt right and we took the plunge.

The plate went up and we were now committed to what I definitely considered to be a lower form of medical life than that of a medical missionary which was the life to which we thought God had called us. A few friends graciously put their lives in our hands.

One of them, Leo, a well known hotelier in the town whose life had been radically changed through his contact with MRA and who was now boldly trying to run his business under God's direction, invited us to set up a health clinic in one of his hotels, just down the road from us, which already boasted Turkish Baths and the like. This proved quite a pioneering venture. People came from all over the country to stay in the hotel and to be given a physical overhaul. A physiotherapist, nearing retirement, offered her services and another doctor gave us an electrocardiogram — a very generous gift. As the local hospital was installing new X-ray equipment, Ken took over their old one which enabled us to do chest fluoroscopy. We must have been among the first GPs to be so equipped.

I was able to add a little to the family income by taking on a few local authority well-baby and ante-natal clinics in the town. My only training for this was sitting in on two sessions with the doctor currently running them, who wanted to give up. The rest I learned on the run from the very competent and patient clinic nurses. I was to have three more babies myself over the next few years, working almost up to the day before and returning to work as soon as I felt able. No one seemed to mind much what I did. Statutory postgraduate training and such matters as maternity leave were still far in the future.

CHAPTER 22

It was not long before something happened which was to be the story of our life for many years to come. People tended to believe, with commendable faith, that, as we were both doctors, their psychologically disturbed friends would be helped by living with us. It was also thought that, as part of this therapeutic process, they would be able to supply me with the help they were sure I must need but could not afford. I never felt as sure about this as they did and even less as time went on.

The first of these was an unmarried lady with very firm ideas on the bringing up of children. The two little girls, Jean still a baby, shared a room and at night I would leave the bedroom door open and a light on in the hall outside. Elizabeth was still not a very good sleeper and easily frightened. Our new 'mother's help' took a strong stand on this. We were spoiling the children with our softness. The door was shut and the light put out. The children wailed and, as soon as the coast was clear, I reopened the door and put on the light again. I was far too scared to confront her for fear of starting off something which we could not handle. It was clearly not an ideal answer to the situation and we had everything to learn. Fortunately the lady soon abandoned us without having been much helped I'm sorry to say.

Two weeks before Christmas 1948 Christopher was born. It was a long and difficult forceps delivery which only added to the joy of cradling this firm, warm little head, which had caused so much trouble, in the palm of my hand which it fitted perfectly.

At home the two little girls were in the throes of whooping cough. Injections against this came into being the following year. The idea of taking a new-born baby

85

into a house where such a potentially life-threatening illness was going on was an anathema to the medical staff as it was to my parents. They wanted me to take Christopher over to them till it was safe to return home. But it was Christmas and, although Ken's much loved sister, Joy, was with them, it felt like a betrayal to abandon them at such a time especially when they were unwell. I asked God what to do and received a quiet conviction that it was right to go back to them. Ken backed up my decision.

We took him home on Christmas Eve. It was dark and the Christmas tree in the town was ablaze with lights. Back in the home Elizabeth and Jean were allowed to gaze at their brother from a safe distance and, with great difficulty, I held myself back from hugging them. That evening the excitement was too much for everyone. It drove Ken and Joy to go to bed early and fall asleep immediately. It kept the small girls wide awake with Christmas expectancy late into the night.

With Ken and Joy out of action, it fell to me to act as aid to Father Christmas and plant the rattling, bulgy stockings on the children's beds. I sat on the edge of my own bed to keep myself awake, feeling distinctly postnatal and increasingly creased in my middle. It was finally around midnight before the delicate manoeuvre could be carried out and I could tumble into bed feeling not a little resentful at my snoring spouse.

When I was feeding Christopher in the safety of our bedroom the girls were allowed to watch from the door. Every now and again a small face would turn puce and a little figure vanish out of the door in a paroxysm of coughing. One morning, Elizabeth put her head round the door and said in a solemn voice she used when she was being especially holy, 'God says you don't need to

worry about Christopher getting whooping cough.' It
was more than adequate reassurance for me.

CHAPTER 23

We now had to get down to work in earnest. Taking over more of the house — and a less convenient one to run would be hard to find — we were able to turn our bedroom into a consulting room while patients could wait in the drawing room. The family was forced back into a partitioned-off area with a very small sitting and dining room combined and a very small dark kitchen which looked out on to a brick wall. Fortunately there was a good sized garden at the back and a playroom-cum-dormitory at the top of the house.

My life over the next few years was spent oscillating between the sink and the surgery. Patients could turn up at any time and we dared turn no one away, so if Ken was out doing visits and the door bell rang I would whip off my apron, run a comb through my hair, shut the children in behind the partition, scramble into a white coat, graciously admit the patient, deal with them and return to the job of getting lunch. We did manage to rise to a once-a-week cleaning lady, dear Mrs. B., who never tired of telling me that polishing furniture consisted of '5% polish and 95% elbow grease.'

Washing machines were still in their cumbersome infancy. We could not have afforded one anyway. Disposable nappies had yet to be invented. The house did not boast anything so luxurious as an airing cupboard so airing of nappies and other laundry had to be done in front of the sitting room fire or over the gas stove in our tiny kitchen. Failing to turn off the gas under the frying pan before attending to a patient on one occasion resulted in a fire which consumed a line of baby's nighties and nappies and most of the paintwork on the low ceiling. Smoke covered the rest. At least we got the kitchen and sitting-room decorated on the insurance — a job which otherwise might have been postponed for many years.

Just as in the camp, it did not take long to discover that there is usually more to a patient than meets the eye. Every GP finds this out sooner or later. Ken became aware of this rather sooner than most. Psychosomatic medicine is now recognised as a respectable idea but in those days very few doctors seemed to be thinking in that way. Paul Tournier was a notable exception but we had not yet heard of him.

Ken's attitude was a constant and uncomfortable challenge to my soft dealing with people. He never hesitated to jump in at the deep end to suggest what he thought might be the emotional or spiritual origins of, for example, a person's stiff neck or gastric ulcer. He was not afraid to bring God into his consultations whereas I found myself, in spite of my Calcutta experience, all too conscious of what the patient might think of me if I did. A few, but only a few, seemed to be offended by his approach. There was one lady who, sitting down abruptly on the chair facing him, said, 'I am suffering from constipation and I don't want any of your God stuff.'

Bournemouth is a beautiful seaside town. 'Health and Beauty' is its motto but, at that time, underneath its sunny surface, we soon found much anxiety and depression; poverty living next door to wealth. Several fine old Edwardian houses had been taken over by the Council to house displaced people from the bombed industrial cities. Still looking grand on the outside, in some of them we found families living in one room with only a small paraffin heater, no proper cooking facilities and having to share a toilet and bathroom with others.

Then there were the elderly folk looking for a warm, tranquil retirement who found rooms in Bournemouth's smaller hotels. They were welcomed in the winter but, as summer approached, the hotel keepers, quite naturally, wanted to make room for the tourists. They needed the extra money and the right holiday image. In the spring we would get a stream of old people coming to our door in great distress and anxiety, not knowing where they were to go for the summer months or how they could afford the higher prices.

Others came south looking for an easier, warmer existence. One was a middle-aged northerner whose wife had chronic nephritis. He had taken over a small guest house, thinking that, with staff to clean and cook, his wife could stop struggling and be waited on for a change. They found, instead, that with staff too expensive to employ, they both had to slave from early morning till late at night to keep things going. Needless to say, he too became ill. One bright spot was the generosity and compassion of the local social services when they were alerted to the situation.

But many unhappy patients came back time and time again. Sometimes Ken would see them and sometimes it fell to my lot. Some of them made us feel very helpless and no one likes that. I can still in my memory see a certain lady walking up to our door and thinking, 'Oh no! Not her again!' When it reaches that stage, something needs to be done.

As well as problem patients on our doorstep, we continued to fall prey to the unfounded faith of many friends that, if only their problem acquaintances could live with us for a while, they would find all the answers they needed, medical and otherwise. This was very complimentary to us but we were totally inexperienced in this sort of thing.

It came to a head when one lady arrived with a great

deal of luggage, put herself to bed and stayed there. She soon demanded, and fortunately paid for, the windows of her room to be hermetically sealed. All her meals had to be carried upstairs to her and all her intimate needs attended to, by me, of course. There was no one else to do it. One memory which still haunts me is of our three year old son standing outside her room with tears pouring down his face when I abandoned him in order to answer her imperious call. He doesn't appear to have suffered any lasting damage. I think I suffered more.

Fortunately she decided she was not receiving the necessary level of attention and took off one day in a vast private ambulance bound for a suitably expensive nursing home. We sighed with relief but, at the same time, with a considerable sense of failure.

CHAPTER 24

All through, of course, our eventual five children, the two girls plus three boys, had continued to occupy a major place in our lives. Thanks to them we rarely, if ever, needed to look outside for our entertainment. This was just as well as we would have had little time for it. All we had to do was to watch or listen. The fun we got from them was like yeast in a lump of dough. It still is, and now we have the added entertainment of grand-children.

They had their moments. The most placid of them, Graham, could be whipped up into devastating fury. His mouth would open like a letter-box and emit an ear-shattering roar. On one such occasion he did fourteen shillings and sixpence (1950s value) worth of damage in the playroom while his two brothers, who had successfully goaded him, took refuge in another room.

Having learned ourselves the immense value, not only in times of stress but at any time, of listening to God, we longed for the children to discover this. The age difference made it easy to pack them off to bed at staggered intervals and this meant that each child had time on his or her own with one of us, rarely both.

We followed a pattern at these times of saying, 'Thank you' to God for the good things which had happened during the day followed by 'Sorry' to Him or to each other for things which had been not so good. Then we would have a time of quiet to give God an opportunity to put any thoughts He might want to give us into our minds.

We left it to the particular child to decide when this time was up. Our dog, for many years, was a large Alsatian-Labrador cross called Brutus. It was his delight to join our youngest at these times. He would hurl the top half of his great body on the bed and remain absolutely still until the final 'Amen' when he would leap off with much tail-wagging.

I look back on these bedtimes as something very rich. There was always a great sense of peace with any rough edges of the day being rounded off. This was after I realised I was often spending much of this precious time planning what I would do when it was over, such as the family ironing or the darning of socks, of which there was always a pile in those far-off days of wool.

These times could sometimes show practical results. One evening, the son being put to bed was quiet for a longer time than usual. I was curious and asked him what he had been thinking about. 'Well', he replied, 'I had just said, "Cheerio, God", when He said, "Hey, hang on a moment!". 'What did He want you to hang on for?' I asked. 'Oh, nothing much', said our son. 'Only something about work at school being important.' His school report recorded a marked improvement halfway through the term!

It is only too easy as a parent, teacher or doctor to force one's opinion on others especially if the situation seems to require an instant answer.

So it happened one day that we were due to go to a wedding. A friend, Sally, from Glasgow, was to marry into a well-known local family. We knew that few of her relations would be able to afford the journey south, so, having a certain amount of Scottish blood in our veins, we decided to show our support by having our eldest, Elizabeth, aged 10, dress up in her kilt. I placed my order and expected her to get on with it.

But although Elizabeth enjoyed dressing nicely she did not like to be conspicuous. Just as we were about to leave the house, with, as usual, only minutes to spare, she emerged from her room looking like a thunder-cloud. Her kilt was undone, her blouse unbuttoned and her hair ruffled. She made it clear that dressing up like that was the last thing she wanted to do.

With a desperate eye on the clock I felt like shouting at her to do as I told her, but wisdom came to our rescue. Instead, wondering if we would ever get to the wedding on time, I told her to go back to her room and ask God what He would like her to do. If He told her to wear a dress that would be all right with me.

She appeared a few moments later, blouse and kilt done up and her hair beautifully brushed. We hurriedly shut up the house and climbed into the waiting car. My curiosity then got the better of me and I asked her if she had asked God and, if so, what He had said? With a serene look on her face she replied, 'He said, "I think it would be nice if you thought about Sally."'

Trying to please everyone can be a desperate business as I well know. Elizabeth one day was faced with just such a crisis. A certain girl at school, whom I shall call 'Paula', was a bully and very unpopular. We had talked about this at bedtime and had decided to pray for Paula. Her parents were divorced, her mother had married again and now there was a new baby boy in the family. It seemed that Paula was probably suffering from a justifiably bad case of jealousy. Elizabeth decided to be friends with her and set about doing this. The result was that she was invited to Paula's birthday party.

The day came and, in the afternoon, six of Elizabeth's school friends turned up unexpectedly to play. Within minutes a 'house' had been constructed on the flat garage roof and there they all were when, as the time for Elizabeth to go to the party drew near, I went out to call her to get ready. The scorn of her friends, when they heard where she was going, knew no bounds. 'Whatever do you want to go there for?' they said. I shouted up to them that Paula needed loving. 'She gets all the love she wants,' commented the eldest girl scornfully. They all thought Paula was spoilt. The girl was, I noted, wearing the badge of the 'Crusaders', a Christian youth group. 'You should know what I mean,' I said to her. Elizabeth stood by, looking miserable.

I went indoors to pray desperately for inspiration. Suddenly I had an idea. I went back into the garden — they were still hanging about indecisively on the garage roof. 'Supposing I make up a picnic for all of you, would you all go?'

The response was immediate, though what Paula's mother would think I had no idea. By the time I had rustled up some sandwiches the garage roof was restored to normality and everything tidied away. Within minutes they were off.

By the time I thought the party should be over, it was raining heavily, so I sallied out with a variety of raincoats and umbrellas. Somewhat fearfully I presented myself at Paula's home but when her mother opened the door the noise coming from inside sounded comfortingly merry. Paula's mother was all smiles. 'I hope you didn't mind,' I said. 'Certainly not,' she replied, 'it was the nicest thing that's ever happened to Paula.'

It did not end there. The girls decided to start a 'Friendship' society. They set about making badges and Paula was elected the first 'honorary' member. Needless to say, that was the end of the bullying.

I did not really believe in using bed as a punishment but, on one occasion, my fury got the better of me and I packed a furious boy off to bed. Some time later, when

I had cooled down, I went upstairs. A lump at the bottom of the bed under the bedclothes was the only indication that anyone was there. I knelt by the bed and said I was sorry I had lost my temper. The lump gradually wriggled its way up the bed, an arm emerged and wrapped itself round my neck. There is no experience in life that can match feeling forgiven.

CHAPTER 25

Through these years we never thought of going on holiday. There was no deputising service in those days and locums were too expensive. Fortunately we lived only a few minutes' walk from the sea and most week-ends would see us piling into a car to make for the nearest bit of the New Forest. As Ken could never contemplate an unproductive outing, however beautiful the scenery, we went armed with shovels and sacks for the collection of pony manure for the garden, 'dunging' we called it.

These excursions were not without their exciting moments. One afternoon our youngest, Malcolm, then aged two, instead of swinging successfully to the other side of a fast-flowing stream, was left dangling from a rope which Ken had thrown over a convenient branch. He hung there philosophically until a suitable branch was found to haul him ashore. Our Jack Russell terrier, however, was so concerned that he fell into the water and had to be rescued further downstream.

For many years Ken and I taught First Aid to the staff attached to the local railway station. Our reward for this was a first class ticket once a year for one of us and two children to anywhere in the UK. We took full advantage of this even if time was limited. Ken once took the boys to the Isle of Coll, which he is proud to think of as the original home of his ancestors. One morning, while they were away, the postman delivered a sheep's scapula, duly stamped, with the address written on one surface and messages on any other reasonably flat area.

On another occasion, finding I could escape for forty-eight hours, I and four children and the aforementioned dog — Elizabeth by this time had left home — took a train to Glasgow, bussed out to Loch Lomond, occupied two neighbouring 'bed and breakfasts' in Liss, spent the whole of the next day in a hired boat on the loch and caught the night train home, spread out comfortably, if unwashed, in our first-class compartment. Just as we were dropping off, an unbelieving, irate lady pushed open the door and asked if we knew we were occupying a first-class compartment. Our reply that we held first-class tickets caused her to slam the door rather unceremoniously and we went back to sleep. We felt as though we had been away for a month.

But it became increasingly difficult to escape from the demands of patients and the continuing succession of needy people who came to stay with us. It was now that Ken felt that God was telling him to 'go and learn all that man can teach about the mind,' and started looking for a job in a mental hospital. Sadly, by this time, he and I had stopped telling each other the thoughts which we felt came from God. We had both continued to spend the first minutes of the day being quiet, praying and listening for anything God might wish to say to us, but Ken got bored with my long-winded, profound and, so I thought, spiritual thoughts, and I was getting to feel irritated by his long lists of practical things to do. We stopped letting each other in on what we were thinking.

Because of this I did not know until many years later that Ken believed that the idea of studying psychiatry came from God. I thought it came from a close female friend of ours whose opinion Ken seemed to value more than mine. The small green worm of jealousy had wriggled its nasty way into me. I did not recognise it as such of course − the last thing we do is to call these things by their right names − but I felt left out and cold-shouldered. I had married a surgeon with a fascinating job and had seen myself at that time as a budding physician working romantically at his side. Now, albeit in the inferior sphere of general practice, we were working well together as a husband and wife partnership. I certainly had not married a psychiatrist and would have thought more than twice about doing so. This was a world I had no wish to enter.

But the real soreness came from seeing someone whom I had considered my friend now being apparently more in his confidence than mine. You can never hide things from children and I was brought up with a jolt one evening. Kneeling by Jean's bed, I said our usual prayer, 'Please, Jesus, help us to be the people You want us to be.' It had a pious ring about it because what I really wanted was that God would do something about Ken. As I tucked her up and kissed her, Jean said, with real anxiety in her voice, 'You would never divorce Dad, would you?' I tried to reassure her by telling her what we had promised when we got married, a condition which for us was binding, and said we were sorry if we had made her worried. I turned to God once more and decided, with His help, to give Ken full backing in his plans and to go on enjoying my friend as I had done before. Although I continued to dislike the situation, the sting went out of it.

The job was found and one miserable autumn day I drove Ken to the fifteen-hundred-bed hospital forty miles away. The day before, I had for the first time seen Ken cry. This had done little to cheer me up. Now the sight of the hospital was enough to make anyone weep. It looked remarkably like the warehouse in which we had been locked up during the war — a huge redbrick building with barred windows, uncarpeted stone corridors with walls painted glossy green or brown and endless locked

99

doors. Anti-psychotic drugs were still in their infancy and violent patients had to be closely guarded for their own safety and that of the world outside. Fortunately the grounds were extensive and very beautiful with a farm on which patients could work and the children could wander whenever we visited Ken there.

Ken, now in his forties and with his past experience of being totally in charge of a busy hospital in China plus several years of general practice, now found himself a junior at the bottom of the hierarchical pile. This was anything but easy for him. One of his jobs was the routine check-up of patients and here his experience stood him in good stead, although his apparent interference, though approved of by the nursing staff, was not always appreciated by his superiors. Many patients had been in the hospital for years, some almost forgotten by their families. Their annual check-ups were often little more than a formality. Ken found himself questioning several diagnoses to find that a significant number appeared to have simple treatable physical conditions which could have had a bearing on the mental problems which had put them there. There were others he felt could be helped by dealing with their underlying spiritual problems. In his first year he managed almost to empty one ward. This was somewhat upsetting to the hospital statistics and was not popular. However, unlike me, Ken never was a popularity seeker. Unexplored territory remained a bait and trespassing a delight.

This job lasted four years during which he was allowed time off to attend courses. When free he would come home at weekends usually laden with fruit and other foodstuffs left over from the doctors' common room to be pounced on by his expectant, hungry family.

CHAPTER 26

With Ken away I found myself totally in charge of what was now a single-handed practice. It was a heady experience but too costly. Various people nobly moved in to help, including for a time Ken's eldest sister, herself a highly trained nurse who would have preferred dealing with the patients rather than coping with housework and cooking. As I had grown to enjoy doing these things, even if my standards left much to be desired, I found it hard when, to her, they were undesirable chores. The one thing she did enjoy was being left alone with the children which, of course, happened very often, and they seemed to have much more fun with her than I ever had time for. She also, quite naturally, disciplined them when she considered it necessary. I felt my position as 'Mum' being eroded. Being a mother now became even more important to me than my dream of being a successful doctor.

For me those years are a blurred memory of transporting children to and from school, taking surgeries twice a day, fitting visits in between, reading to children and putting them to bed. I clung to my right to do this. Night calls did not worry me too much. Ken had usually done them, but I found it much easier to get up and go myself than it had been waking Ken up and keeping him awake after the telephone had rung.

I found the early hours of the morning a fantasy time when one could feel a little mad, with no traffic and the car headlights reflected from dark, empty shop windows. Once at 2.30 am I succumbed to the temptation I had often had to drive round the main roundabout in the town the wrong way. My pulse raced as I expected to clash head on with a ghostly police car but all was well and I retired satisfied to bed.

It was a vulnerable time of the night too, especially for a lone female. In those early days we were the proud possessors of an elderly Lanchester car, a rare breed and one of the first to have automatic gears. On a dark night by the town cemetery the engine stopped and nothing I could do would coax it into going again. I was about three miles from home and did not fancy walking that distance along deserted streets. I sat and prayed, longing to be home in bed.

It is my experience that angels come in many disguises. The silence of the night was suddenly broken by the sound of raucous singing as three men came in sight, swaying arm-in-arm down the middle of the road. As they came near, one of them broke away and lurched towards me. I sat tight and prayed even more earnestly. Through the window he yelled, 'Wha's the matter?' Winding the window down an inch, I told him and when he learned it was a Lanchester he roared with laughter. 'I've worked with them for nine years,' he guffawed. Up went the bonnet and after a moment's tinkering, it was banged shut again. 'Now try,' he shouted and with one turn of the ignition switch the engine leaped to life. With a cheery wave of his hand and another burst of merriment, he staggered off towards his companions and the trio vanished into the darkness.

An old friend now took over to act as receptionist, mother's help and anything else that might be needed. With Ken away we were able to clear the house of extra inhabitants. My dislike of Ken going off was partially mollified by the feeling of satisfaction at being the doctor in charge with all our patients dependent on me.

General practice has its dramatic, alarming and miraculous moments. No other branch of medicine can

102

quite match it. I was called, one day, to a patient with a high temperature and difficulty in breathing and swallowing. As I was supporting her in my arms to make her more comfortable, it suddenly hit me that she could be suffering from a particularly nasty form of poliomyelitis and here I was in very close contact. Having seen her safely off to hospital, I dashed home, found a bottle of Dettol and gargled furiously. My diagnosis was sadly confirmed but I was none the worse.

On another day I was just about to turn the car into the road when I caught sight of my friend in her white coat waving frantically on the doorstep. She had just taken a phone call from a woman to say that, having had an urgent feeling that she should leave work and go home, had found her husband unconscious on his bed with an empty bottle of sleeping tablets at his side.

By the time I arrived he was not only unconscious but had stopped breathing. He was sprawled face downwards on the large double bed, his legs partially blocking the doorway so that it was all I could do to squeeze myself into the small room. There was no way in which I could attempt textbook resuscitation. All I could do was to clamber up on to the bed, straddle his back and pump his chest until the ambulance came — the longest twenty minutes of my life. He made a complete recovery and was convinced that God had saved his life and was deeply moved by the whole episode, as was I.

A certain lady, who always wore a straw hat with flowers on it and rode a bicycle round the town collecting all the free literature, brochures and the like, which she could lay her hands on, came to see me with an infected corn on one of her toes. Having dressed it, I told her to keep it dry. A month or more later she returned. 'I have done as you said,' she announced. 'I haven't even taken my stocking off.' Before I had even removed her shoe, I was fully prepared to believe her. It took ten minutes of a wide open window before I dared invite the next patient in. Miraculously the toe had survived.

CHAPTER 27

When, after a year, it became clear that Ken would never return to general practice, we decided that I should take on a partner and gradually let him or her take over. This happened very easily. I selected a young man and, as it was his first job in general practice — no such thing as vocational training — I enjoyed my last chance to feel big as I broke him in. Being a competent young man, he needed very little help from me.

Giving up the practice would involve moving away from the immediate area. Not everyone approved. One woman seemed ready to take me to court over it, asking how I could possibly consider moving away when I knew her mother needed me. Too bad.

The next question was where we should move to. We had recently acquired a small copse in the New Forest which Ken had seen advertised in a magazine in the doctors' mess. It was going cheap because the former owner had been refused building permission. We bought an aged caravan to put on it and this became our escape at weekends.

One day, when driving to the copse, we passed a house for sale and all of us thought, 'That's it!' It was just the right size for the family. We put in one bid after another but each time we were outbid. Sure that we were on the right track and encouraged by our friends, we stretched ourselves to the absolute limit of our resources, but we still did not win. We wondered what God was up to.

Two or three weeks later, while Ken was away on a course, the agent wrote to say that a lady who owned a house not far away from the one we had wanted had heard of our disappointment. Would we like to look at hers? She had no plans to put it on the market so there was no one else after it.

Jean and I, really to oblige the kind lady, went over on a late misty October afternoon. For some reason I was expecting an ivy-covered Victorian house which I was sure I would not relish. Instead we were totally bewitched by what we found. The house, three times the size of the one we had originally gone for, was set in the heart of the forest with a stream running through the garden. We were met by the sound of trickling water, one of my favourite sounds. It would be way beyond our reach financially and it hardly seemed worth going in. However we did and were duly shown around. I was captivated by the walk-in airing cupboard — no such thing existed in our present house — but when I saw the number of rooms I thought, 'If God does want us to have this house, what on earth does He expect us to do with it?'

We finally came to the crucial question which I thought would hit the nail on the head and I could hardly believe my ears when she mentioned the exact figure to which we had previously been stretched. There was to be no bargaining up or down. She would leave curtains and carpets and there was no hurry. Her only condition was that we did not have a cat and she was quite fierce about this. We discovered very soon that it was indeed a bird sanctuary which would not go well with cats. Five months later we moved in.

By the time this happened Ken had moved to a hospital nearer home but by now was getting more and more impatient with the restrictions of being a junior doctor with limitations on the time he should spend with patients and the emphasis on drugs in treating them. One day, as he was walking through a ward, he passed the bed of a patient who was curled up under the bedclothes out of sight. He had no idea who she was but felt moved to slip his hand under the blankets and stroke her head. There was no response, but next day he met a girl in the corridor who told him that she had felt perfectly well after he had touched her. This incident made him long even more to be free to work in his own way. The problem was that he had a family to support.

There is a hymn which says that 'God moves in a mysterious way His wonders to perform.' Extricating Ken from hospital work was one of His most mysterious. He received an invitation to work with a South African doctor who was partially sighted but had trained in manipulative skills. He was setting up a private clinic in a nearby town and suggested that, while he dealt with the physical side of patients' needs, Ken could tackle the psychiatric side. The pay would be way above anything the Health Service could offer and a car would be included in the deal. This was a carrot Ken could not refuse. He handed in his resignation and started working in his new luxurious surroundings.

The promised car was not immediately forthcoming and we were surprised to find it up for sale in a local garage. As we needed a new one and Ken's pay was good, we bought it. But from the start there seemed something strange about the man although he had been accepted by the local Masonic Lodge without question. Out of curiosity I looked him up in the Medical Register and his name was not there. With suspicion growing I made for South Africa House in London. There was no record of his ever having attended Cape Town University as he had claimed or being on any medical list. This was worrying as it was an offence to be in partnership with an unqualified practitioner. One day Ken saw the 'blind' man walking briskly along the road with obviously no impairment of vision. He decided to get out as quickly as he could. He announced that he was planning to work separately from home and his lawyer sent out printed notices to all his patients, plus one to the local press, dissociating Ken from his 'partner'.

How we were going to manage to support the family we couldn't see, especially as I had not yet found any work in our new already over-doctored area. It was a large-sized step in faith, but no sooner had we taken it than the 'doctor' vanished with his wife, their car being found abandoned on Poole quay. On Ken's first independent day at home, a patient asked to see him and from that day they never stopped coming.

CHAPTER 28

So opened a new chapter in our lives. From now on the house would never be empty. Most of those who came had already been through the psychiatric mill. One had been seen by nineteen psychiatrists before she came to Ken as a last resort. He was now able to combine his psychiatric training with his own approach to people's underlying problems. Time was limitless. Many travelled some distance to reach us and before long we found ourselves obliged to keep them for as long as it was necessary and I soon saw the reason for the large number of rooms in the house. Some stayed overnight, others for several years, becoming close family friends.

Ken, always on the lookout for things that might be useful at no cost, had managed to help himself to an ECT (electro-convulsive therapy) machine which the hospital was throwing out in favour of a new one. It worked perfectly well and he used it, when appropriate, for several years. On these occasions, as a general anaesthetic was involved, I was required to stand by and assist.

A few patients were apprehensive about this treatment though very appreciative when, after the third time, they suddenly felt their spirits lift and life seemed worth living again. One lady positively revelled in coming in yet again for ECT. As the anaesthetic began to 'take', she would open her mouth to its full capacity in a great yawn and say, 'I'm going!' then, with a blissful smile relapse into unconsciousness.

I heartily disliked the whole procedure. In fact, I am ashamed to say my dislike of psychiatric illness increased the more I saw of it and I resented its invasion of our home. My heart fell every time I opened the door to yet another pale, unsmiling face, only to be overcome with guilt at my own reactions when, miraculously, most of them left looking pink and happy. Interestingly we noticed a distinct difference between the selfish and the unselfish. The depression of some would throw a heavy cloud over the whole house while others, equally affected, would suffer within themselves casting no shadow of gloom.

Though not always possible we tried not to have more than two patients in residence at any one time. This was important both for the patients' sake and, even more, for the family. We all had to live and feed together and there were still four children left at home, the youngest only seven. Amazingly they appeared totally unaffected by the sometimes strange behaviour of our visitors. They seemed to take it all very much for granted and this certainly helped in the rehabilitation of lonely, isolated folk.

The dog exerted a very definitely therapeutic influence. To him, human beings were just human beings and God's gift to dogs, and he loved them all, taking them for walks in the Forest and unfailingly bringing them back again.

Our amateur status came to an abrupt end when, one day, a man, mildly depressed, who was to be with us for a few days, suddenly went berserk and we were obliged to get him into hospital. This came to the ears of the Medical Officer of Health who fortunately knew us slightly. He descended on us and told us in a firm paternal way that we could not have people staying in our house for purposes of medical treatment unless we were registered as a nursing home.

This meant calling in the police, who advised us to leave all doors open at night so that the dog was free to roam, and the fire brigade, who told us to keep all the doors shut. We were also to be inspected at regular intervals by a doctor who would question the inmates on the quality of my cooking, examine the contents of the fridge and test the workings of the loos. The latter were of an old-fashioned nature unfamiliar to the retired consultant who came. When he tried to hold the chain out at right angles it naturally did not work and this was reported to the authorities. We asked that, next time, an inspector should be sent who understood these finer things.

One day it all suddenly became too much for me. I was trying to prepare a meal when one of the children wanted me to find a lost something immediately, Ken wanted a letter typed out that very moment, one of the patients was standing by me pouring her problems into my ear and the telephone started ringing. No one else made any move to answer it. I left it ringing, dashed upstairs and locked myself in the bathroom − blessed place of retreat! − 'How much am I supposed to take?' I shouted inwardly at God. 'Just as much as I care to give you,' was the unexpected response, but the thought seemed to come, as it does so often, with a smile and I found myself laughing.

I returned to the kitchen. The chaos was still there but it didn't seem to matter any more, and each component quietly sorted itself out. I understood at that moment that the cause of so much stress-induced ill-health is basically the resistance we put up to the endless challenges of life, the 'I can'ts' and 'I won'ts'. No resistance, no stress.

CHAPTER 29

I had hoped, when we moved, to be able to have a limited list of patients of my own. In our old practice patients had seemed quite genuinely pleased to see me. In the '60s women doctors were still quite a rarity and I modestly thought what an asset I would be to any all-male practice. However, the response from the local doctor to whom I wrote was far from warm. I was informed that I was entering an already over-doctored area and that any attempts on my part to get in would be firmly resisted.

Somewhat deflated I had settled down to a year of being a housewife, largely on my own all day, except for our young Alsatian-Labrador cross of a dog, with no medical work apart from the occasional immunising sessions in school to keep my hand in. The children continued to go to their old schools, so Ken would drive the twenty-five miles to his hospital each morning dropping them off at their various schools on the way and picking them up again on his way home in the evening.

For the only time in my life I had the leisure to stand still, undisturbed, at the kitchen window watching the birds. I had always been glad to see the birds in our old garden, but now with a bird table just outside the window I was able to get to know them as individuals. There were hundreds of them and I began to understand why the former owner had insisted on no cats. Some, like robins, blackbirds and thrushes, I knew, but nuthatches, greater spotted woodpeckers, dunnocks, marsh tits, coal tits and many others were new to me. On the river were mallards and moorhens, the infrequent heron and, most wonderfully, the occasional flash of the brilliant blue of our own kingfisher. A bird-book became my most constant companion.

It wasn't long before I became a sufficiently familiar object for the tits, a little warily at first, to eat out of my hand. There is nothing which quite equals the thrill of feeling tiny wild claws perched fearlessly on the palm of one's hand.

I had been assured by townspeople, who thought they knew, that it would be twelve years before we would be accepted into the village community. Not to be put off by this, I decided to contact the local Women's Institute, the bulwark of any British village. In those days one had to be nominated and then approved before being allowed to join. I approached the local secretary in her picture-book thatched cottage and she graciously agreed to introduce me. It quickly became and still is a major part of my life.

The other way to 'get in', I thought, was via the Church. The little 12th Century parish church stands at the far end of the village. The vicar at that time was a very dedicated ex-Brigadier who rode round the parish on horseback. It was the days when ladies wore hats and services were still restricted to Prayer Book Matins and Evensong with the Prayer Book Communion service somewhat thrown in at the end of Matins for the few who wanted it. It was all very foreign to me and, as recognition after a service was a matter of a polite 'Good morning, Mrs. So and So', it did little in terms of getting to know anyone reasonably well.

As a Non-Conformist, I was not officially permitted to take Communion in an Anglican Church and, as I had joined my old church at the time God had first become real to me, I felt no need for further 'confirmation'. When I approached the Brigadier on the subject, he said,

'My dear girl, I could no more refuse you than leave a child outside the door with a party going on inside.' Thirty years later this same church feels more and more like an extension of my own family. Gone are the hats and formality. Children, once frowned on, skip merrily down from the altar after being blessed and nobody complains.

A year passed before a friendly neighbour introduced me to her GP who promptly invited me to join him and his partner in their practice as a part-time assistant. This arrangement was to last for twenty-five years. At first, being the first woman doctor in the area, I was something of a novelty and the men, being of a chivalrous nature, could not bring themselves to expect me to do night calls. I told them that, being a mother, I was probably more used to getting up at night than they were.

Part-time it had to be as the demands of cooking, cleaning, children and patients in the home continued unabated. Sitting peacefully in the surgery a few times a week, concerned with only one person at a time, came as a welcome respite. On the days I was being a 'doctor' a good friend would trundle over on her moped, come wind, come weather, to take on the domestic side. She was also a keen gardener and, with the help of patients, a rough piece of ground was turned into a productive vegetable plot. Water was a problem as it had to be bucketed out of the river and carried up a steep slope, much being lost on the way, but it all proved excellent occupational therapy.

One of these patients was a retired missionary who had burnt himself out with overwork. When he first arrived, and for a few months afterwards, he would hold on to the back of a chair, trembling with anxiety before daring to venture out of the house. He finally spent many hours digging out the totally resistant couch grass to create the vegetable patch and, as he dug, hurling stones merrily in every direction, only narrowly missing a recumbent patient sunbathing on the lawn below. His appetite came back, his face assumed a healthy tan and his humour returned as his spirits rose. He eventually managed to walk as far as a nearby Methodist Chapel where he began to take Bible classes and became a much loved figure. After two years or so, now into his seventies, he was able to take on work as a member of a clergy team in a busy Midland city church. He undertook the bulk of the visiting in the Parish, keeping two bicycles always available for the purpose in case one broke down. It was said that, by popular demand, he conducted more marriages in the parish than any of his colleagues. The vegetable patch had fulfilled its mission in more ways than one.

CHAPTER 30

The area served by the practice to which I was attached contained a rich mixture of farms, docks and industry. The spectrum of patients was much wider than in our old practice but the needs of people were just the same as they had been there, or in the camp for that matter. People are people wherever and whoever they are and our main claim, if not our only claim, to equality is our need of help. It took a while for patients to accept that it was safe to be seen by me rather than by their well trusted, familiar male doctors, but I only remember one man who, on opening the door and seeing a woman, put his hands over his eyes and exclaimed, 'Oh no!' Those days have long passed. Women, at the time of writing, make up about fifty per cent of the intake into medical schools.

But some things never change. General practice is still particularly good for keeping one on one's toes. One never knows what will come through the door next. It may be a baby who, as his mother said in broad Yorkshire, 'pumps up', or a young man with 'saddle boils', a condition it took me a while to understand until he explained that he was a marathon cyclist. It might be the elderly man complaining of loss of vision who simply needed to have his glasses cleaned or the overweight lady who swears blindly that she 'never eats anything'. Just as you are indulging in a little light humour at your patients' expense, the next to come through the door could be – and was – a nine year old girl brought by her father because of a swelling on the arm which he thought was an unpleasant but innocent insect bite but which was, obvious at once to me, going to prove a very nasty malignant growth. She died a few months later. I never found it possible to be emotionally detached.

Perhaps, because I was a woman in an all male practice, I seemed to receive more than my fair share of women suffering the physical or mental effects of stress in the home usually caused by having to live with a difficult or unfaithful husband. Occasionally it might be a man having to live with a difficult or unfaithful wife. They sometimes seemed to find it less embarrassing to cry in front of a woman. Then there was the man who turned up suffering from shock having arrived at work only to be told that he was no longer needed, made redundant without even so much as a 'thank you' or a 'sorry' after thirty years of service, and the lady suffering real bereavement after the loss of her beloved cat. All these are part of the everyday fare of the GP and our training does not always prepare us for them.

Patients rarely come with these matters at the top of their agenda but with a full range of symptoms and complaints from raised blood pressure to tummy aches. It was usually the innocent question 'Is everything else all right?' that opened the floodgates to the real need.

So often I longed to be able to write a prescription for faith — a knowledge that there was a God who loved them and could tell them what to do or how to react. But in dealing with such problems, or the often more difficult ones of under-age girls demanding the Pill or perfectly healthy women demanding abortion, I now had to consider not only the reaction of the patient, as in our own practice, but also the reaction of my colleagues who were also my bosses. I was, after all, as an assistant advising their patients, their source of income. It was teasing that I feared more than full-blown disapproval.

For a long time I trod very carefully, until, at last, the urgency of many people's situations drove me to fling caution to the winds along with my reputation. Fortunately my colleagues proved to be very long-suffering and I was allowed to continue with them until well after retiring age.

It always took a conscious act of will to get involved at a deeper level. I was aware of the emotions which might be released and the time it might take with others waiting. The strange thing was that, when I did leap over the barrier of unwillingness, I would find a concern for the patient which hardly seemed my own, with the right questions being asked and the answer given in far shorter time than would have appeared possible.

So many problems of this kind seem to boil down to the 'me first' syndrome. So many miserable, ill women would assert, 'I have a right to be happy', or 'I must think of myself.' I would think if only she would stop doing just that, how much better she might sleep and how much more attractive she would look and therefore how much less likely that her husband would need to seek satisfaction elsewhere. Some of them did, and the change in their appearance was remarkable as were the stories they told of altered conditions at home when they reported back. One lady's face, however, remains fixed in my memory. 'Forgive?' she shouted. 'You are asking me to do the impossible,' and she left the room taking her misery and her depression with her.

CHAPTER 31

I continued to find the lessons I was learning day by day on the home front very useful therapeutic tools, not that I always had to talk about them, but they certainly helped me to understand my patients better and possibly to pass on the prescription for the answer. Doctors cannot be expected to experience every ill in the book but any ache or pain which I have had myself has helped me to be more sympathetic. They have all had their uses.

Patients sometimes helped me too with their faith and often with great courage and resilience. They could help practically as well. One of my temptations has always been to eat too much. My greed was a source of worry to my mother, especially the time she found a plateful of chocolate cakes, put out for a large tea party, empty, with me standing nearby, chocolate smeared round my mouth. I knew what a battle it could be to say 'No.' So, when a patient seriously needed to lose weight and we had investigated the reason, I would suggest that when she was tempted to nibble or have a second helping she should think of me and I would think of her when similarly tempted. It worked well for both of us.

Not always, though. One afternoon I paid a surprise visit to an elderly lady for whom I had suggested a diet as she was grossly overweight and her heart and joints were complaining. I found her consuming a large cream bun. When I remonstrated with her, she said she thought it was all right as long as she ate it between meals!

The most difficult patients to deal with were those demanding termination of an unwanted pregnancy when I could find no physical or mental reason for agreeing. I am old enough to remember the days when to aid in any way with an abortion was to risk being struck off the

Medical Register. It was a relief to have firm guidelines. It is true that it could be hard work supporting patients though the despair of the first few weeks, but by the fourth month or so the child would be accepted and the pregnancy would end in delight.

One mother particularly comes to my mind. An already anxious character in her late thirties, her eldest daughter was also pregnant. Embarrassment added to her fear and unwillingness. Today it would have been difficult to refuse her longing for termination. However, she was perfectly healthy and the pregnancy posed no threat to her life — the only grounds at that time on which abortion could legally be performed. By the fourth or fifth month she and the family had become used to the idea and the baby girl was warmly welcomed by her and her husband on whom she greatly depended. When the girl was twelve her father suddenly died. The rest of the family had long since left home and her mother told us she did not know how she would have coped without her thoroughly sensible and loving youngest daughter.

Overnight in 1967 the situation changed and now anyone opposing abortion was to be labelled 'lacking in compassion'. I found this very hard to take, as my heart ached for the often distraught girl or woman under enormous emotional pressure and faced with such a choice. I always felt that I had two patients to consider, if not three if one considered the father. Having been pregnant five times myself and aware how soon one knows one is that way, I had always felt that the foetus was in fact a baby to be recognised and accepted into the family from the word 'go'. Now we were discussing doing away with him or her. I could never feel dispassionate about this and nor, apparently, could the mother.

Now, of course, we know far more about the sequelae of abortion. It seems bound to leave its mark physically, mentally or emotionally. My husband's recent work has established a link, as yet not well recognised, between an abortion in the family and mental disturbance from pseudo-epilepsy to large numbers of cases of anorexia nervosa occurring in other members of that family. All the same, within a ten-minute consultation time, faced with a woman, often a girl, under great pressure from mother, grandmother, boyfriend or the demands of her job, holding on to what one really feels is right and therefore best for everyone in the long term can be a daunting business. I found the simple expedient of saying as unemotionally as I could, 'You mean you want me to arrange to get rid of your baby?' was often enough to make them change their minds. One of my colleagues who had changed his mind about easy access to termination said, 'There's nothing so satisfying as watching a group of Mums who had wanted to abort their babies gloating over their young as they roll around on the floor.'

During these years, I felt I was getting the best of all worlds — working with Ken, fully involved with my home and village life, plus the opportunity to do what I always longed to do — practice medicine.

CHAPTER 32

As Ken had more and more people passing through his hands, most of whom had failed to be helped by orthodox psychiatry, he began to take more notice of what they were telling him. Most bizarre statements made by mentally ill people are written off as the fantasies of a sick mind and treatment is aimed at suppressing or minimising these symptoms, but Ken began to take them seriously, a fact much appreciated by the patients themselves.

One of these was a young woman school-teacher who, at times, would withdraw into a silent world of her own from which it was impossible to rouse her. She would emerge from these 'absences' to appear quite normal. She had been examined and treated by numerous psychiatrists without effect. As she gained confidence, she owned to having a long-standing lesbian relationship. Her friend had died and, during these 'blackouts', which dated from her death, she was actually, in her mind, reliving her lesbian experience. She felt 'taken over'.

Ken asked the help of a friendly vicar who, at a specially arranged service, ordered the 'possessing' friend, in the Name of Jesus, to leave the woman alone. The patient described the sensation which followed as having felt there was a hole in her head through which something got out. She never had a repeat of her attacks and shortly afterwards got married and became a Sunday School teacher.

Other patients appeared to be controlled by non-human entities, evil in nature. Many of these had a history of involvement in occult activities often starting with apparently innocent playing with ouija boards or Tarot cards.

These experiences coincided with quite an upsurge of interest in the occult and Ken soon found himself linking up with others, especially priests of various shades, who firmly believed in the possibility of demon or devil possession, and who practised exorcism in a Christian setting. Once he was asked by a fellow psychiatrist to help with a woman who seemed beyond the help of ordinary treatment and it was discovered that her husband had been involved in occult practices. On another occasion he was called to an army school in Germany where occult goings on had been discovered leading to quite serious disruption. For a few days he was delighted to find himself an honorary Major in the British Army.

So concerned were some Church leaders at that time that a committee was set up to investigate and Ken was invited to be on it. Meetings were held in utmost secrecy for well-founded fear of 'attack' from those they were investigating. Ken, though taking it all very seriously, with his youthful delight in exploring forbidden territory rather enjoyed the cloak and dagger aspect of it all.

For me it was yet another excursion into a world I would rather have had nothing to do with. In some cases, though certainly not all, I wondered whether 'demons' were being blamed for what appeared to me to be ordinary human sin needing to be recognised and forgiven. I feared once more for the direction in which Ken seemed to be heading.

All these years I had continued to be involved in the activities of Moral Rearmament which, to me, seemed to be the spearhead, or one of them, of Christianity in the world, with its constant expectation of miracles in the lives of difficult people or situations. It often meant going to London or elsewhere for meetings, helping to organise conferences and the like. To Ken all this appeared to be very much less important than the work he was doing. His teasing made me feel belittled and quite genuinely concerned on God's account too.

Debating rather fiercely with God about all this one morning, the thought came, 'You must give Ken absolute freedom to follow his own path.' Then, to my surprise, came the added thought, 'To go to the dogs if that's what he chooses'. How much more freedom can you give anyone than that? There was yet another thought to come — 'Follow Me yourself'. I realised that I had, once and for all, to stop trying to mould Ken into what I thought he should be and which might make life more comfortable for me.

I said nothing to Ken but immediately things seemed to be different. I stopped worrying about what he was doing and his teasing of me ceased abruptly. I thought, 'What a good girl am I!'

So it was with considerable surprise that, a few weeks later, I heard Ken tell one of his patients that 'three months ago, Frances and I decided to give each other absolute freedom to do what we felt was right.' And so it has continued to this day and Ken has not yet gone to the dogs!

CHAPTER 33

One subject on which Ken and I have always agreed is the children, that is, how wonderful they are. We have tended to be mildly scornful of other parents who considered theirs to be equally special.

The way we treated them during their growing up time was not always the same. He, as father, was quite rightly the main disciplinarian, to the point when the noise the children were making with their bawling at his hands was worse than the trauma they had caused by their misdemeanour. I would stand helplessly by, being a 'peace almost at any price' sort of mother.

He also had a way of press-ganging the entire family into doing jobs or going to places none of us particularly wanted to do or go to and it was strangely impossible to refuse. We would grumble and sweat but, when the job was completed and he had stood back and said with pride, 'I never thought we would manage it', or after an exciting, adventurous outing, we would feel that perhaps he wasn't so bad after all.

However there were times when I, taking the family along with me, seemed to be on one side and he on the other. This bothered me and I mentioned it to a friend one day. She thought for a moment and then said, 'He probably thinks you care more for the children than you do for him.' Into my mind came a picture of him coming home from work, having collected the children from school on the way. I was so fussed about getting them fed and down to their inexorable homework that I virtually took no notice of him, not even stopping to say 'Hello.' No wonder if he felt excluded.

So many times I have been grateful for the remarks of friends which have switched on a much needed light.

One particularly valuable piece of advice came from another friend when I complained to her that on some points Ken and I did not see eye to eye. I innocently thought that husbands and wives who considered themselves to be Christians should be totally at one in everything. We were walking along a cliff top overlooking the sea, a view riveted in my memory, when she said, 'If you try making oneness with your husband your objective, you will never find it. Make your oneness with God your priority and everything else will come as a by-product.'

The other thought, long embedded in my memory, was the one I had when driving away from our wedding reception wondering whether our marriage would work: 'Change is always possible.' I developed the practice, when my voice had risen to a harsh soprano and Ken's language had inevitably become rather less than polite, of sitting down and asking God, 'What's wrong with me?' There was no need to ask what was wrong with Ken, it was so patently obvious – to me anyway. The result was, again, always like the switching on of a light and I would see why I had reacted the way I had and what I might have done or said, or more likely not done or said. The whole situation seemed to take on a different colour and peace was restored. I used to say 'sorry', imagining that was the correct thing to do, but it had to happen so often and only re-ignited Ken's irritation, so I dropped it and decided, with God's help, just to be different. We both now know very well when the other is sorry without anything having to be said.

The children too, over the years, have provided wholesome insights into our behaviour. Once, when our eldest was small, in a fit of frustration, I smacked her. The blow was intended to land on that part of the anatomy destined for that purpose but, because of her wriggling, it landed in the middle of her back and winded her. I said I was sorry and that sometimes she was bad and I had to help her not to be and sometimes I was bad and she had to help me. 'Yes,' she said through her sobs, 'that's what you've got a little girl for.'

On another occasion when I must have been, as I thought, exercising my maternal right to speak on matters of right and wrong, one of our sons said, 'I always know when you're moralising, Mum.' It apparently had a hollow ring about it.

For a while, when she was all of two years old, we were concerned about the criminal propensities of our second daughter. We were sure she must be helping herself to food from the larder and, sure enough, one day we caught her in the act. She was standing with her back to us clad in her hand-me-down pink dressing gown which was too long for her and clutching something in her hands. Her head was down and her eyes were tight shut, presumably so that we wouldn't see her. In her hands, prised open with difficulty, was a cold potato. As I pondered on her behaviour, I had a vivid picture of myself idly helping myself to the odd sultana and leftovers thinking of them as nothing more than Mother's perks. I told her about this and we both stopped forthwith.

On the whole we survived the 'teens' remarkably well, but there were a few anxious moments. One of the boys would disappear with the local gang and we had no idea of where they were or what they were doing. If they came to the house, they would walk through the kitchen past me without saying a word and shut themselves in the sitting room. My imagination would run wild wondering what noxious plans they were hatching.

I developed a very real fear of losing my son's confidence and of the trouble he might get into. I didn't dare intrude or ask any questions.

When I eventually referred the matter to God, the thought that came was, 'Be his Mum.' I had a picture of myself, as I had sat many years before, holding a struggling, bellowing little boy on my lap as he viciously kicked my shins, until the struggling gradually ceased, the thumb went into his mouth and all was tranquillity.

The next time the gang appeared they looked rather glum, so without any of the usual apprehension or holding back, I found myself asking what was the trouble. They didn't seem to mind my interference in the slightest and said they were all going to a party which entailed each of them having a girl in tow and they were one girl short. I then proceeded to mention all the girls' names I had ever heard mentioned, each one being crossed off for a variety of reasons till the whole business became hilarious and I was never afraid again.

There were other times when, communication not being very good, we sometimes worried about just what they might or might not be doing. One day, as I was driving, I was praying in the sort of way that feels like clinging to God's skirts, thinking I was thus protecting them from evil, when the thought leaped into my mind — it seemed as though it started with 'For goodness' sake' — 'Stop praying worriedly and miserably. Pray hopefully and expectantly.' It immediately made me feel different, as though I was handing over the responsibility to God and, on this particular occasion, unexpected positive things certainly followed.

CHAPTER 34

In the '70s Ken's work took a giant leap forward. We had stopped taking patients into the home, partly as we felt we had had enough and partly because the authorities were tightening up their regulations. They now insisted that we box in our staircases and fit new fire doors in various places. We were very loath to institutionalise the house in this way. Our decision to de-register also made it possible for us to see off our last patient, a schizo-phrenic youth who looked like settling in for life.

But patients continued to come and consult Ken in increasing numbers and their often bizarre symptoms or the 'voices' they heard took on a new significance for him. He had in the past been aware of the possibility of 'possession' by some dominating friend or member of her family, alive or dead, and had labelled this the 'Pos-session Syndrome'. Now, in addition, he began to suspect other influences from the family past.

He was almost shocked into this by being asked by an Anglican priest if he could advise about his niece who was in a mental hospital. She was a young mother who had developed a terrible urge to gouge out people's eyes, especially those of her children. She was considered sufficiently dangerous to be kept locked up in a padded cell.

Ken commented that this had a very medieval ring about it. The priest replied that this was hardly surprising as she came from a family who had owned a castle in which, in days gone by, people had been tortured and this was known to have included the gouging out of eyes. Ken had once visited this castle as a tourist and knew that in the middle of the dungeon floor, was an oubliette, a hole through which the prisoner could be pushed out into the moat below. In the middle of the patient's cell was a two-inch drain-hole which she saw as the entrance to her coffin. It all tied up, but what then?

At this point the priest suggested consulting the local Bishop who without any hesitation offered to hold a Requiem Mass for the family. To Ken, with his Nonconformist upbringing, this was foreign language, but he went along with the idea and the service was planned for the following weekend. That very evening the hospital phoned the patient's husband to say that his wife had suddenly, for no known reason, appeared absolutely normal. He could safely take her home. As if this was not enough of a miracle, two weeks later a message was received that an aunt of the patient who had, unknown to Ken, also been in a mental hospital, had also unexpectedly recovered that same day and her husband had taken her away for a holiday in Italy.

Since then and up to the present time, Ken has followed the same pattern of investigation and treatment with patients suffering from mental disturbance or physical complaints which have not responded to orthodox treatment.

Having made sure that the patient has already had a thorough physical examination, he proceeds to examine the family tree, drawing it out in as much detail as the patient can provide. This often means including the wider family to collect all possible information. He then looks for anyone in the family who has died unmourned or uncommitted, being especially concerned to identify anyone who has died a violent death such as in war, murder or suicide.

Increasingly significant, especially in relation to Anorexia Nervosa, are aborted babies or miscarriages who have not been wanted or recognised. Many of these are held as shameful secrets by the patient's family and it may be with much pain and difficulty that they are brought into the open. Often the 'voices' heard by some patients or their behaviour or complaints help to identify the lost individual whom the patient may seem to be imitating.

Having identified them he then encourages the patient with other members of the family to hold a service, preferably in the context of the Eucharist (Mass or Holy Communion) during which the individual is committed to God and forgiveness is sought for the wrongs surrounding his or her death. Amazingly, when this has been carried through faithfully, patients have recovered, sometimes immediately, sometimes over a longer period.

To me, at first, it was yet another excursion into unwelcome territory. It seemed even further removed than some of his earlier ventures from the basic ills, emotional and spiritual, with which I found myself faced. Normal human sin I could understand, with its need for repentance and forgiveness. Some of his ideas I did not want to believe and some I could not. Once again I feared where it might lead him and how far it might separate us.

By the mid '70s he felt he had enough evidence to write a book. My heart failed. Quite apart from the contents, writing is not something Ken finds easy. Or rather, he thinks everyone else makes it too complicated. He fails to see the point of such details as full stops, capital letters or paragraphs. Trying to make something readable out of his writing is like unravelling spaghetti. Several people, including a journalist friend and two young Jesuit priests, had a go and it was finally handed over to a professional 'ghost' writer who produced a highly readable book, *Healing the Family Tree*.

I am ashamed to say that I hoped, and even went so far as to pray, that the book would never get off the ground. I thought that people would think Ken was mad and that the same would go for his wife as well. However, once again came the thought to give Ken his freedom, so this was one prayer of mine that was apparently ignored.

The book was published in 1982 and within a year had become a best-seller and is now in several languages with others on the way. For many people around the world it has proved a life-saver and the gateway to faith. It has taken him around the world lecturing and interviewing people of all sorts. A Hindu mother in India had a vision of Jesus during a Eucharist being held for her schizophrenic daughter who, although many miles away, was cured at that time. He has joined in prayer with First Nation Americans and Australian Aborigines in healing some of the wrongs of the past. He has since written two more books in which more of these stories are told.

If God wanted someone to get this idea off the ground then He could not have chosen a better person than Ken to do it. Perhaps we need a little 'madness' in this modern age of reason and unbelief.

CHAPTER 35

It has always puzzled me that some athletes should actually choose to be hurdlers when they could run on the flat and get to the finishing-line faster and with less effort or risk of bruised shins. I can only suppose that they find it more challenging and satisfying.

In life there are the brave few who seem to seek out hurdles to leap over — mountaineers for example — and, even braver, members of the rescue services or bomb-disposal squads. But, for all of us, hurdles of a rather different sort seem to be our lot and come, for the most part, uninvited. Endless decisions and choices face us daily. We have to make up our minds from a very early age whose side we are going to be on and who we are going to try to please. It often involves taking risks — risks of making mistakes, risks of failure, losing friends or being unpopular. Then the hurdle we mostly try to dodge — living with difficult human nature. We may be humble enough to be worried about our own nature but if so we are probably already on the way to getting over this hurdle. Most of us, I suspect, are much more bothered by other people's annoying tendencies, especially if we have to live or work in close proximity to them.

I am not the most willing of hurdlers. I would far rather run on the flat. There have been many times when I have been put off jumping for fear of what might be on the other side, often for no other reason than that I have broken something which Ken valued and I am scared of owning up. I've even been driven to telling the odd white lie — if lies are ever white. It's only left me feeling a failure.

The trouble is, the longer one puts it off the higher the hurdle seems. One time it took me over a week and the hurdle seemed higher with every day that passed. Someone had said something which hurt in a way few things have. I said to myself, 'You're a Christian so of course you should forgive.' This was followed by a small voice in my ear whispering, 'Why should you?' Immediately I felt consumed by resentment. If I looked happy how would the offending person know they had done anything wrong? On the other hand, looking glum was not likely to impress them either. Meanwhile I felt miserable. Praying was impossible. Failure to jump can have tragic consequences. One person we knew had been badly hurt and decided she would avoid all relationships in future which might involve further hurt. She died, an elderly lady with no friends even to go to her funeral.

On the eighth day I could stand it no longer and finally asked God what I should do. 'You can drop it as soon as you choose,' was the answer. I realised I was clutching my resentment to my breast as if it was my most precious belonging. All I had to do was let go. Whether the other person was wrong or not was entirely between them and God. For my part all that mattered was that I was right with Him.

People ask: how does one know if thoughts come from God? I can only say that these thoughts are always surprising — not something I would be likely to think up for myself. They are quietly compelling, never bossy or harsh. They are always positive and fit in with Christ's teaching as we have been given it. They often come with the feeling of a smile behind them. After all, God wants the best for us and for us to get the most out of life. Obedience to the thought is often the only test of its truth. It seems to be part of our creator's plan to allow us to have hurdles to leap over. Many of them, probably

134

the vast majority, are of our own making, but even deciding to live His way does not seem to exempt us from them. Perhaps it is the only way to develop our spiritual muscles and keep us fit and growing.

The family is the ideal setting for such healthy living, though not the only one. However, if parents and children can prove the possibility of 'change' within the family they have a valid recipe for coping in any situation. It is the ideal workshop for life in the outside world. That is maybe why God, as underlined by Jesus, thinks it so important.

Ken and I are both approaching the finishing line. It may be many years away or it could be just round the bend. Who knows? It has been a race mostly exhilarating, occasionally frightening and sometimes exhausting, but never boring. There have been many, many enjoyable flat bits between the hurdles with our full quota of fun, but each hurdle that has faced us has been worth jumping and seems to have landed us on a slightly higher plane with a better view. Well over fifty years since the day when I wondered if it would work with two such different characters we are still married and more thankful to be so than we can say.

When I mentioned the possibility of writing this book, Ken remarked, 'Well, we should certainly have something to say about sticking together.' That gave me the all-clear to go ahead. I had been prompted by the tragedy of so many people today who seem to give up, often at the first hurdle, especially in marriage. I asked someone who was living in an uncommitted relationship whether she disapproved of marriage. Her answer was that she had seen so many of her friends get divorced after a few months or years that it hardly seemed worthwhile even trying. Another girl said she had no intention

135

of going through the hell her parents went through. It seems to me that we have been brainwashed into thinking that struggle or sacrifice in any area of life should be avoided wherever possible. Our rights and our happiness have become our gods, to be constantly placated.

We are happy to be part of the evidence that marriage does not have to be hell nor does it need to break down. In our case it becomes warmer and more tranquil as the years go by. We still have to jump from time to time but the hurdles do not seem so high these days and the distance between them seems greater. There will doubtless be a few around to the end of our days to keep us from becoming too complacent. We still do not agree about everything, but have discovered that love is not dependent on agreement. It's a matter of going ahead and loving regardless.

The hurdles along our way have, for the most part, been those which everyone faces in the course of normal life and probably all of us have had our own less usual ones to jump. From our own experience, and from what we have witnessed in the lives of people who have faced infinitely higher hurdles than we ever have, we have come to the conclusion that there is no hurdle so high that God cannot give us the strength and the know-how to jump if we ask Him.